ALSO BY WITOLD RYBCZYNSKI

Now I Sit Me Down

Now I Sit Me Down

FROM KLISMOS TO PLASTIC CHAIR:

A NATURAL HISTORY

Witold Rybczynski

FARRAR, STRAUS AND GIROUX

NEW YORK

Farrar, Straus and Giroux
18 West 18th Street, New York 10011

Copyright © 2016 by Witold Rybczynski
All rights reserved
Printed in the United States of America
First edition, 2016

All illustrations are by the author.

Library of Congress Cataloging-in-Publication Data
Names: Rybczynski, Witold, author.
Title: Now I sit me down : from klismos to plastic chair : a natural
history / Witold Rybczynski.
Description: First edition. | New York : Farrar, Straus and Giroux, 2016. |
Includes index.
Identifiers: LCCN 2015041604 | ISBN 9780374223212 (hardback) |
ISBN 9780374713355 (e-book)
Subjects: LCSH: Chairs—History. | Sitting customs—History. | BISAC:
ANTIQUES & COLLECTIBLES / Furniture. | ARCHITECTURE /
History / General.
Classification: LCC NK2715 .R93 2016 | DDC 749/.3209—dc23
LC record available at http://lccn.loc.gov/2015041604

Designed by Jonathan D. Lippincott

Our books may be purchased in bulk for promotional, educational,
or business use. Please contact your local bookseller or the Macmillan
Corporate and Premium Sales Department at 1-800-221-7945, extension
5442, or by e-mail at MacmillanSpecialMarkets@macmillan.com.

www.fsgbooks.com
www.twitter.com/fsgbooks • www.facebook.com/fsgbooks

1   3   5   7   9   10   8   6   4   2

In memory of Michael Graves

All men recline for rest, and must walk about upon their errands in this world. Yet how they sit, during ceremonies, while eating, or in their hours of labor and leisure, is what distinguishes them from their neighbors; and this distinction we feel deeply somehow to be fundamental.

—George N. Kates, *Chinese Household Furniture*

A chair is only finished when someone sits in it.

—Hans J. Wegner

CONTENTS

Now I Sit Me Down

Introduction

I own a creaky old wooden office chair that swivels, tilts, and rolls. I bought it in a flea market more than thirty years ago to use as a writing chair or, rather, as a typing chair, for at that time I used a Hermes portable. My first computer was an Osborne, followed by a succession of PCs, each more powerful and more versatile than its predecessor. Now I write on a Mac. The Osborne is stored in an attic cupboard, although I'm not sure why I hang on to it. *Valore sentimentale*, the Italians would say. My Osborne has a monochrome screen the size of a postcard, uses an obscure computer language, stores information on plastic floppies, and runs obsolete software. In other words, it is twenty-three pounds of useless junk. On the other hand, my old office chair is still usable. It's a so-called banker's chair, with a scooped seat, curved arms, and a contoured back, a design that first appeared in Edwardian England. You won't find other artifacts from that period in my home—no antimacassars or spittoons, no gasoliers or Victrolas—yet my banker's chair continues to do its job.

A chair can be a living link to the past. Even the distant

past. I would feel odd wearing a Greek chiton, and I wouldn't know how to consult the sibyl of the oracle at Delphi, but like Achilles and Odysseus I can sit on a klismos, the ancient Greek chair. The one I recently used wasn't a precious antique but came from JCPenney. That's not unusual. Ours may be a digital age, but we continue to manufacture and use period chairs: wing chairs, rocking chairs, Windsor chairs.

There is good reason to copy the klismos—you have to jump ahead more than two thousand years to the English cabriole of the eighteenth century to find a chair of equal elegance. Other candidates might include a Louis XV armchair, the fin de siècle Viennese café chair, and the mid-century modern Eames chair. And there are many lesser useful chairs: club chairs, reclining chairs, deck chairs.

Chairs are fascinating because they address both physiology and fashion. They represent an effort to balance multiple concerns: artistry, status, gravity, construction, and—not least—comfort. Chairs can be whimsical or blandly practical, luxurious or simple, a frill or a necessity. My short history chronicles many changes in chair design, but unlike communications equipment, transportation technology, and weaponry, which have become more efficient, faster, and deadlier over time, chairs do not necessarily get "better"; some models persist unchanged for centuries. On the other hand, chair design is not static. Change is caused by the availability of new materials, by new social conditions, by new production methods, and by new uses. It is also caused by new fashions as well as the desire for novelty, and periodically by spurts of the inventive human imagination, which is never satisfied to leave "well enough" alone.

As chairmaking evolved from individual craftsmen, to guilds, and finally to industrial production, the responsibility for design shifted. Since the nineteenth century, many chairs have been designed by architects. This was largely a result of the Arts and Crafts movement, in which architects designed furnishings, wallpapers, lamps, even table services, to complement their interiors. Like a building, a chair combines artistry and function. Unlike a building, however, a chair's fate is at the mercy of its users. A building may turn out to be unpopular or impractical, but once it is built we are stuck with it—demolition is only rarely an option. A chair, on the other hand, is different; if it is disliked it will be set aside, manufacturers will discontinue making it, and it will soon be forgotten. But if it garners favor, it—or rather its design—can survive for centuries. Banker's chairs continue to be made today, as are bentwood café chairs, and many Danish Modern chairs. Unlike most consumer goods, chair models can have a long life; some never go out of fashion. Or, like the JCPenney klismos, they reappear to function just as their original makers intended.

This book is not a conventional design history; it is as much a chronicle of human behavior as of human artifacts. The first chapter traces the evolution of the simplest sitting implement—the stool—and shows how every period copies or adapts what came before, all the way back to pharaonic Egypt. Next, an overview of domestic furniture reminds us that there are many kinds of chairs because there are so many different reasons to sit. This leads to a theme that is a constant in my story: the chair is a practical tool, but it can also be an aesthetic object—cherished, admired, even collected. Finally, there is nothing natural about sitting on chairs—after all, many societies prefer to sit on the floor. Why do we sit up on chairs? The story of how the ancient Chinese switched from floor-sitting to chair-sitting sheds light on this matter.

The middle portion of the book traces the story of the chair from prehistoric times to the present day. It does not attempt to be comprehensive but touches on the high points: the progression of the simple side chair from a glorified stool to the refined British cabriole chair; the golden age of sitting furniture in Louis XV's France; the appearance of exemplary folk models such as the English Windsor chair and the American rocker; the saga of Michael Thonet, who invented the long-lasting bentwood café chair; the advent of the modern designer, whose work was separated—for the first time—from actual chairmaking; the mid-century Danish Modern movement, which combined traditional craftsmanship with factory production. Individuals make an appearance: Thomas Chippendale, author of influential furniture handbooks; the *ébéniste* Jean-François Oeben, who raised furniture-making to a fine art; the first designers, such as the turn-of-the-century Viennese architect Josef Hoffmann; the Bauhaus maven Marcel Breuer; Charles and Ray Eames, who pioneered chairs in new materials; and the Danish master Hans Wegner. These individuals are a reminder that chairs often involve invention as well as artistry, and that new solutions are produced not only by circumstances but also by creative minds.

The final chapters explore special chairs. Chairs that fold—safari chairs, director's chairs, lawn chairs—are so ubiquitous that they are almost invisible, yet portability and chairs emerged hand in hand in ancient Egypt and dynastic China. Knockdown furniture was developed simply for ease of transport but has ended up as a marketing phenomenon. We think of swings as children's playthings, but swinging seats likewise have ancient roots and have persisted in the form of porch swings and gliders. Finally, chairs on wheels, whether for infants or invalids, demonstrate how human ingenuity can adapt an everyday object to special uses.

While we continue to use chairs based on historical models—chaises longues, easy chairs, rocking chairs—two dissimilar chairs represent our period's particular, one might say peculiar, contribution: the recliner and the ergonomic task chair. While one is used mainly for watching television and the other for desk work, both are based on a systematic study of the human body and represent new solutions to age-old problems: people come in different sizes, and comfortable sitting requires that we are able to easily alter our position. In both chairs mechanical adjustability provides an answer.

Chairs are affected by—and reflect—changes in technology, materials, and economic and social conditions, yet they remain intimately connected to peculiarities of the human body—after all, we sit on them. At the same time, chairs communicate a lot about our attitudes—toward comfort, toward status, toward our physical surroundings. They are inanimate objects, but they speak to us. What they say is the subject of this book.

ONE

A Tool for Sitting

François Boucher is best known for his idealized paintings of beguiling odalisques and cavorting maidens, and for his languorous portraits of his patroness Madame de Pompadour, but my favorite Boucher is a domestic scene. A pair of women is sitting by a window in a small but elegant room, the boudoir of a Parisian apartment. A servant wearing an apron has just finished pouring hot chocolate from a pewter pot; you can see the steam rising from the cups. He probably brought the drink from a nearby shop, for bunched carelessly on the mantelpiece is the napkin in which the pot was wrapped. The lady of the house, a delicate beauty wearing a morning gown and a makeup cape, is offering a spoonful to her little son. Her companion, a young nursemaid, is holding a baby girl. It is a charming depiction of an intimate family moment—the embodiment of bourgeois domesticity.

Boucher painted *Le déjeuner* in 1739.* He regularly

---

*In modern French, *déjeuner* refers to luncheon, but in eighteenth-century France it meant breakfast—as it still does in French Canada today. Boucher's painting is sometimes called *Family Taking Breakfast*, or—mistakenly—*Morning Coffee*.

used his wife, Marie-Jeanne, and their children Juste-Nathan and Elisabeth-Victoire as models, and the setting is likely his own home. The room embodies tasteful but not luxurious comfort, and delights in visual effects. The large pier glass set into the paneling above the fireplace reflects a doorway and a divided portiere, or door curtain, a common feature of fashionable homes. The walls are decorated with sea-green crackle-painted paneling and gilded rocaille moldings. The pale morning light pours in through the tall window, but one can imagine the room in the evening, flickering candlelight multiplied by the gilded moldings and the mirror. The rocaille decoration, the chinoiseries, and the shapely mirror frame signal the advent of rococo taste—a new fashion. The decor was likely designed by Boucher himself, for, in addition to being a successful painter, he was also an accomplished decorator.

The boudoir is full of *stuff*: a delicate red-and-black lacquered tea-table, a gilded console table, a pair of candle sconces, an ormolu wall clock, oriental knickknacks, porcelain cups and saucers. "In effect, the only tokens of history continually available to our senses are the desirable things made by men," observed the Yale art historian George Kubler in his classic *The Shape of Time*. "Of course, to say that man-made things are desirable is redundant," he continued, "because man's native inertia is overcome only by desire, and nothing gets made unless it is desirable." It was Kubler's thesis that desirable things not only mark the shape of time—in his happy phrase—but whether they are an opera by Rameau, a play by Molière, or a painting by Boucher, they also provide us with a window on the past.

Boucher documented a time when visual delight was combined with practicality. The eighteenth century excelled in furniture, and while the two caned side chairs in the painting are plain by the luxurious standards of the time, they look comfortable and the caning makes them light enough to be easily moved—the furniture arrangement near the window looks like a last-minute improvisation: "Let's have our chocolate over here."

The Humble Stool

Boucher's little boy, who is holding a pull toy in the shape of a little horse—another desirable thing—is sitting on a low stool. Actually, it is a *repose-pied*, an upholstered footstool, but it serves him perfectly well as a seat. Stools are the simplest form of sitting furniture. There are several in our home: a counter-height stool in the kitchen, a low stool in the bathroom, and a pair in the dressing room. The stool in my study has been piled high with books for months, but that doesn't matter—it's only a stool. Stools probably first saw the light of day as flat slabs of wood with three pegged legs; three because floors were uneven. Simple stools existed—and exist—in all rural cultures; they are easy to make and serve a variety of uses, from peeling potatoes to milking cows.

In seventeenth-century England, the first everyday chairs were called "backstools," because they were stools into which a straight board had been inset to support the sitter's back. Backstools continued to be used throughout the eighteenth century in rural Europe and America, their lack of comfort made up for by the simplicity of their construction. Such primitive chairs were descendants of the fifteenth-century *sgabello*, a fancy backstool found in the palazzi of Italian noblemen, whose coat of arms often adorned the carved backpiece. A simplified version called a *stabelle* can still be found in homes and country inns in present-day

Alpine regions of Germany, Italy, and Switzerland.

A particular version of the stool that has survived over the centuries is the folding camp stool. Today, such stools are used mainly by fishermen, campers, and weekend painters, but before their adoption as portable seats for recreation, they served a different purpose. Folding campaign stools appear in many Civil War photographs of military encampments. A century earlier, at the outbreak of the Revolutionary War, George Washington ordered eighteen folding stools from a Philadelphia upholsterer for his headquarters; one of these stools is on display at the Smithsonian.

Sgabello, *fifteenth century*

The folding camp stool in the L.L.Bean catalog is virtually identical to Washington's stool except that it is made of aluminum tubes and ballistic nylon instead of wood and leather. The ingenious design has persisted because it is hard to improve. Lightweight and easily portable, with intersecting legs that fold flat when not in use but are stable when unfolded, the X-frame ensures that the fabric seat remains taut no matter the weight of the sitter. The design inspired the form of the starkly elegant stool that Ludwig Mies van der Rohe designed for the German pavilion at the 1929 International Exposition in Barcelona. The leather cushion is supported by straps stretched between polished stainless steel X-frames, although the crossed legs do not fold. In addition to four stools, the pavilion contained two chairs of similar design that were reserved for King Alfonso XIII and Queen

Victoria Eugénie of Spain when they formally opened the building.

The furniture arrangement in the Barcelona pavilion followed historical precedent: Napoleon Bonaparte's throne room at the Château de Fontainebleau has two rows of upholstered X-frame stools, or taborets, but only one chair—the emperor's throne. The striking contrast between Napoleon's throne and the lesser stools is a reminder that status and sitting furniture are never far apart. Throughout history, grander, taller, more impressive chairs have been a mark of distinction, and their use has been a privilege reserved for the select few.

Napoleon's furniture maker modeled the taboret on the Renaissance scissors chair, whose legs were a series of intersecting curved wooden frames that extended up to support armrests. Sometimes the chair was foldable, sometimes not; sometimes it had a flat backrest. Renaissance scissors chairs were beautifully carved, often with expensive inlays of ivory, metal, and boxwood, and were reserved for nobility. When Andrea Mantegna painted *The Court of Gonzaga*, in the 1470s, he showed the Gonzaga family and courtiers gathered on an outdoor terrace. Only the marquis and his wife are seated, everyone else is standing. Her chair is hidden by her voluminous dress, but his scissors chair, covered in embroidered velvet, is plainly visible, as is a puppy lying contentedly between its curved legs. More than four centuries later, when Jacob Ezekiel sculpted the American financier Anthony J. Drexel, he portrayed the international banker and patron of the arts as a latter-day Medici by placing him on a Renaissance scissors chair.*

---

*The statue stands today on the campus of Drexel University, of which the financier was founder.

"Everything made now is either a replica or a variant of something made a little time ago and so on back without break to the first morning of human time," observed Kubler, who distinguished between *replicas*, which were simply copies of earlier devices, and *variants*, which were modifications. The scissors chair was a replica of the medieval faldstool. Meaning literally "folding chair,"

Renaissance scissors chair

this X-frame portable throne accompanied kings, bishops, and other dignitaries on their frequent travels. Faldstools are mentioned several times in the *Song of Roland*; one of ivory, another—belonging to Charlemagne—of solid gold. The oldest surviving faldstool, which belonged to the seventh-century Merovingian king Dagobert, is made of cast bronze. The faldstool was a replica of the ancient Roman *sella curulis*, a ceremonial folding stool used by consuls, senators, and high magistrates. The curule was elaborately decorated and carved and was sometimes provided with arms, but it must have been uncomfortable if used for long periods for it had no back, a feature said to be intended to discourage overlong deliberation.

The curule was a variant of the folding stool used by Roman military commanders in the field—a badge of rank as well as a seat. The Romans copied this stool from the Greeks. Stools (*diphroi*), both folding and four-legged, were a common feature of Greek life and were used by all strata of society—even the gods in the Parthenon frieze sit on stools. A vase painting from the fifth century B.C. shows a woman with a parasol sitting on a folding stool, apparently

Roman curule

taking part in a picnic. A mural in the Minoan Palace of Knossos on Crete, dating from the fifteenth century B.C., portrays several young men seated on folding stools, drinking wine. When the archaeologist Arthur Evans discovered the mural, he christened it the Camp Stool Fresco.

No actual Greek or Minoan folding stools have survived, but fragments of ancient folding stools have been found in funerary barrows in Germany and Sweden, and an intact Bronze Age folding stool was unearthed in an archaeological dig in Guldhoj, Denmark. The X-frame is ash wood and a fragment of the seat is otter skin. Scholars have debated if this stool is a Scandinavian invention, or if, like the folding stools of the Greeks and Minoans, it was a cultural import—a replica. If it was the latter, it traveled a great distance, because, as far as we know, the folding stool appeared first in pharaonic Egypt.

I visit the Egyptian collection at the Metropolitan Museum in New York, where I find two wall paintings that portray men on folding stools. One is from the tomb of a high official and shows him supervising workers on his estate. The other, also from the tomb of a government functionary, depicts a group of young army recruits sitting on folding stools waiting to have their hair shorn. Evidently, the Egyptians used folding stools as everyday outdoor seats—not so different from today's camp stools—and they do not appear

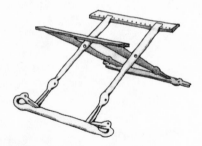

*Eighteenth-dynasty folding
stool frame*

to have been badges of rank; many wall paintings depict
stools being used by workers and artisans. On the other hand,
an actual folding stool that is displayed in another of the
Met galleries was clearly a luxury item: the frame is elaborately carved in the form of long-billed birds and is made of
wood inlaid with ebony and ivory. This stool dates from the
eighteenth dynasty of the New Kingdom (1550–1295 B.C.).

One of the wall paintings that catches my eye shows a
carpenter sitting on a stool, using a bow-drill, with an adze
and square close to hand. He is building a chair. There are
many examples of Egyptian chairs at the Met, with and
without arms, often beautifully carved, usually with woven
cane seats, sometimes with seat cushions, occasionally combined with footstools. Unlike stools, chairs appear to have
been reserved for the exclusive use of important personages.
During the early Middle Kingdom, an unusual type of chair
emerged with a backrest only a few inches high, just enough
to support the pelvis and sacrum, leaving the back free to
find its own angle of repose.* None of these chairs has survived, but judging from graphic evidence it appears that the
backrest may have been padded. This kind of seat appears in

---

*This kind of pelvic support is unique and does not reappear until the late nine-
teenth century—in the tractor seat.

scores of statues, reliefs, and wall paintings of pharaohs, royalty, and other dignitaries. Indeed, the Egyptian hieroglyph for "revered person" depicted a noble seated in a chair. The chair man.

My Chairs

I don't consider myself a collector, but I estimate that over a lifetime I've owned more than sixty chairs. A recent acquisition is a side chair that my wife, Shirley, and I bought last year in a consignment shop. Dating from the early 1900s and vaguely Arts and Crafts in style, it has a delicate tiger oak frame and a caned seat. It is a classic side chair: the front legs are straight, the rear legs are splayed and extend up to form the back, which is slightly angled. The legs are reinforced by delicate stretchers. The chair is pretty to look at but is rarely sat on for it serves as our "bedroom chair," that is, it's where we hang our clothes at night. The twentieth-century Danish furniture designer Hans Wegner once designed a three-legged chair especially for this purpose—not a chair used as a clothes hanger but a clothes valet designed like a chair. The top rail is shaped like a coat hanger to receive a jacket, and when lifted the hinged seat serves as a place to hang one's trousers—and reveals a small tray for keys and change. And you can still sit down to lace your shoes.

Chairs are used in so many different ways. The chairs in my study are handy places to stack books. Chairs are always useful when you have to reach something on a high shelf. Henri Matisse once painted his assistant in his Nice studio using a side chair as an improvised easel. *The Morning Session* shows her working on a canvas that is leaning against the chairback; she has placed her palette on the seat. The easel-chair and the chair she is sitting on will probably soon be used for lunch.

A dining chair is the simplest of chairs. It must be the right height for a table, and it must accommodate a person sitting erect for a limited period of time; it doesn't need much padding, and arms are optional. A dining chair needs to be light enough to be easily pulled up to the table as you sit down—and pushed away as you get up. In the past, dining chairs

Valet Chair
(Hans Wegner)

in grand homes were heavy because there was a footman available to slide the chair under the sitters (waiters in expensive restaurants still provide this service). Our bentwood dining chairs are very light. They're not all in the dining room, there are a couple in the breakfast room and a couple in the sunroom, and they get moved around a lot, depending on how many guests there are for dinner.

I've built a dining table and several desks over the years, including the worktable on which I'm writing this. The maple-veneer plywood top is supported by a maple apron and tapered legs. Its Shaker-like simplicity has less to do with design philosophy than with my limited carpentry skills. While I have occasionally turned my hand to stools and benches, I've never built a chair. "The chair is a very difficult object," Mies van der Rohe once observed. "Everyone who has ever tried to make one knows that." A chair requires strong joints—dovetail, mortise and tenon, finger—and it has to be light enough to move and strong enough to carry a couple of hundred pounds. A well-built chair will support a person tilting back on its two rear legs—although my wife scolds me whenever I do this. Most important, a chair has to be comfortable. It has to allow movement and also provide support in all the right places, which requires subtle curves and carefully shaped slats and rails.

The chair in which I spend the most time is the chair I sit on while writing. A desk chair is more demanding than a dining chair because it has to accommodate a variety of postures: sitting upright to type, leaning forward to consult a book, leaning back to think about what to write next. A desk chair also has to be comfortable for longer periods of time, but not too comfortable—after all, it's a work chair. Thomas Jefferson, who was interested in furniture, had a swivel desk chair when he was secretary of state. "Who has not heard from the Secretary of the praises of his wonderful Whirlgig Chair, which had the miraculous quality of allowing the person seated in it to turn his head without moving his tail?" wrote one observer.

Jefferson certainly qualified as a chair collector. When he returned from his five-year stint as minister to France, he brought back no fewer than fifty-seven chairs. These included side chairs and upholstered easy chairs. The last made ideal reading chairs, for the invention of upholstery in France and England coincides with the rise in popularity of reading for pleasure. A good reading chair must be comfortable, above all, and its design should allow the relaxed reader to become fully absorbed in the printed page. My own favorite is a wing chair. The upholstered seat, back, and sides create not only physical comfort but also the feeling of being in a secluded little retreat. Jefferson's cosy reading chair, which stood in his library at Monticello, was a barrel-shaped easy chair upholstered in red leather.

Watching television is very different from reading. Our attention is focused on a small—or not so small—screen, and we are immobile for several hours, which may be why the chair most associated with television-watching—the recliner—resembles an airplane seat. I don't have a recliner—I use a rocking chair—but like many viewers I like to put my feet up. Although footstools have been used since Egyptian times, the padded ottoman is a relatively new accessory, arriving in Europe in the late eighteenth century from Turkey.* Jefferson, who loved newfangled gadgets, had one of those, too; indeed, his record-book entry—"Paid for an Ottomane of velours d'Utrecht"—is the first written evidence we have of the use of that word in English.

My wife watches television in a chaise longue that resembles a daybed with an adjustable back, although as the name suggests, it was originally conceived as a "long chair," long enough to support the legs—a marriage of easy chair and ottoman. Chaises longues were common in eighteenth-century bourgeois homes—Boucher once painted his pretty wife reclining in a *duchesse*, a daybed with one end designed like an armchair. French chaises longues had a variety of names—all feminine—depending on their precise design: *veilleuse, sultane, turquoise, méridienne*. The recamier had a raised back at each end and is named after the chaise longue in Jacques-Louis David's famous portrait of Juliette Récamier. Such chairs were commonly found in salons as well as boudoirs, and were chiefly used by women. This was not the case with *canapés*, or sofas, which were a variant of the chaise

---

*The ottoman is part of a family of low padded furniture that includes poufs, tuffets, and hassocks, which can be used interchangeably as low seats or footstools.

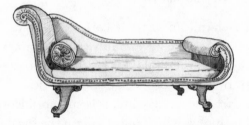

Recamier chaise longue

longue and appeared at the beginning of the eighteenth century. A charming pastel by François-Xavier Vispré shows a young man reclining on a *canapé* while reading a book. He is wearing a casual banyan and bright red slippers, and is stretched out full-length, comfortably propped up by a pile of cushions.

Chairs need to accommodate different activities—reading, writing, dining, socializing, watching television—as well as different postures—sitting up, lounging, reclining. But they also need to satisfy something else. As the architect Christopher Alexander has observed, "What is less obvious, and yet perhaps most important of all, is this: we project our moods and personalities into the chairs we sit in. In one mood a big fat chair is just right; in another mood, a rocking chair; for another, a stiff upright; and yet again, a stool or sofa." This emotional connection occurs because a chair, unlike a table or a chest of drawers, has a personality. It is not only a tool. We choose a hammer—a tack hammer, a claw hammer, a mallet—depending on the job at hand. But as Alexander writes, the job of sitting is not purely functional; it reflects our state of mind. The astonishing historical variety of chairs is as much due to this intimate relationship as to functional imperatives.

An Unusual Tool

The personality of a chair can vary. It can communicate status—"I am important"—like an executive desk chair or an armchair at the head of the table. Or cultural values— "I admire the classical world" or "I like modern design." Because a chair is a part of everyday life, it is susceptible to changing tastes and fashions, which may explain the disappearance of the scissors chair and the periodic reappearance of the folding stool. A chair can also reflect changing cultural habits. The nineteenth-century popularity of rocking chairs, for example, paralleled the sociable custom of sitting on the porch, just as deck chairs accompanied ocean travel and outdoor recreation.

The chair is a barometer of human behavior and attitudes to posture. Do we want to recline, lounge, slouch, or sit upright? Do we seek status or comfort? Or both? The chair answers these questions. It is sometimes an anonymous product, but it can also be the result of an individual's imagination—Jefferson's in the eighteenth century, Mies van der Rohe's and Hans Wegner's in the twentieth.

George Kubler pointed out that works of art can be both the answer to a question and a reformulation of that question.

Every important work of art can be regarded both as a historical event and as a hard-won solution to some problem. It is irrelevant now whether the event was original or conventional, accidental or willed, awkward or skillful. The important clue is that any solution points to the existence of some problem to which there have been other solutions, and that other solutions to this same problem will most likely be invented to follow the one now in view. As the solutions accumulate the problem alters. The chain of solutions nevertheless discloses the problem.

So, too, with chairs. We don't know exactly what led the ancient Egyptians to invent the stool. It may have been something as simple as a need to sit down when performing certain tasks, such as carpentry. We do know that sitting on a chair was associated with ceremonies, and it was likely the need for a portable throne that resulted in the ingenious folding stool. What Kubler called a "chain of solutions" involving status and portability led to the Roman curule and the Renaissance scissors chair and, in a curious offshoot, produced the Hollywood director's chair, a portable seat reserved for the director or star, whose name was prominently stenciled on the back. The chaise longue, on the other hand, was the answer to elegant repose. It redefined posture as half sitting, half reclining, and ultimately led to the sofa and the lounge chair. The chaise longue was ill-suited to the out-of-doors, however—you couldn't drag it out onto the beach. The solution was a folding chair that combined supine comfort with light weight and easy portability: the deck chair. The wood-and-canvas deck chair did not require new materials or new technology. It was loosely based on the Egyptian X-frame stool, but cleverly added foldable armrests and an adjustable back. Watching someone struggling to unfold a deck chair is to be reminded of its intricate geometry.

A complicated little contraption—and something more. The contrast between the hard, scissorlike frame and the floppy canvas defines the character of this mechanical yet carefree chair. The latter quality is underlined by the gaily striped fabric—who thought of that? Even the humblest chair can inspire an aesthetic impulse. Will the armrest be smooth or carved, will the finish be glossy varnish or sparkling gilt, should the upholstery be patterned or plain, ought the graceful leg to curve this way or that? In other words, this is a tool with an artistic dimension.

TWO

If You Sit on It,
Can It Still Be Art?

Beautiful chairs are aesthetic objects, but of what kind? We refer to artifacts such as the ormolu clock and the gilded console table in Boucher's *Le déjeuner* as "applied" art, to distinguish them from the painting itself, which we call "fine" art. The dictionary defines applied art as "the application of design and decoration to everyday objects to make them aesthetically pleasing," a distinction that seems to be mainly a question of function—or its lack. Boucher's painting, which graced the walls of a series of private homes before ending up in the Louvre, provides visual and intellectual stimulation but has no practical purpose. A pretty ormolu clock, on the other hand, is a tool for telling time, just as a caned chair is a tool for sitting.

The distinction between function and aesthetics is not simple, however. Boucher was a painter, but as we have seen, he was also a decorator, and he regularly carried out commissions for tapestries, porcelain figurines, and book illustrations, as well as theater costumes and sets. Jean-Honoré Fragonard was not above painting panels and overdoors as part of interior decoration. The women's dresses that

Antoine Watteau depicted in his idyllic scenes inspired actual fashions, and gave rise to the so-called Watteau pleat. For these artists—and their patrons—the line between art and everyday objects was not hard and fast.

One of the last works of the great cabinetmaker Jean-François Oeben was a dressing table for Madame de Pompadour (now at the Metropolitan Museum). The table is of a particular type invented by Oeben. At first glance it appears to be a simple writing desk with an elaborately decorated top. But the desk contains surprises. Insert a crank, turn it, and an internal clockwork mechanism causes the top to magically slide back and the central portion to slide forward. Two side compartments hold perfumes, powders, and cosmetics. Push a discreet button and a central leather-covered panel tilts up at an angle. The panel has a ledge and can serve as a bookrest, or it can be pivoted to reveal a looking glass. Push another button and a shallow drawer pops out below. The ornamental marquetry of the various parts, like everything else about this exquisite contraption, is dazzling. Pompadour was a great patroness of the arts, and Oeben's marquetry depicts a vase of flowers surrounded by the emblems of her creative interests: a building plan and architectural instruments, a painter's palette and brushes, a musical score, a garden rake and watering can.

Such marriages of beauty and convenience were commonplace in the eighteenth-century interior. Rooms were all of a piece: the floor parquetry, the stucco ceilings, the paneled walls, the tapestries and painted silk wall coverings, the branched candle sconces and chandeliers, and, of course, the furniture. The individuals responsible—the cabinetmakers, upholsterers, varnishers, lacquerers, silversmiths, goldsmiths, and locksmiths—each had their own guild with its own clearly defined responsibilities and apprenticeship requirements. Architects, painters, and sculptors were also part of this team. Art and decor complemented each other: paintings took their place as panels, overmantels, overdoors, and ceilings. Framed paintings and mirror glass were an integral part of the decorating scheme, and architects' drawings indicated their precise locations: flanking a canopy bed, or centered over a console table. None of this is to belittle art, but rather to emphasize that practicality and beauty were not considered mutually exclusive. The marquetry of a dressing table was expected to provide the same visual delight as a painted canvas—and vice versa.

The eighteenth-century novelist and playwright Françoise de Graffigny has left us a firsthand description of a rococo interior. She was visiting a recently decorated country house in Champagne in the winter of 1738, and in a letter to a friend she recorded her impressions of her hostess's *appartement*.

> Her bedroom is paneled and painted light yellow, with pale blue moldings; an alcove of the same, framed with delightful Indian [meaning Chinese] paper. The bed is in blue moiré and everything matches so that even the dog basket is yellow and blue, like the chair frames, writing desk, corner cupboards and secretaire. The looking-glasses with silver frames, everything is wonderfully polished. A large door, glazed with looking-glass, leads to the library, which is not yet finished. Its carving is as precious as a snuffbox. There will be looking-glasses, paintings by Veronese, etc. One side of the alcove is a small boudoir; you fall on your knees when you go in. The paneling is blue, and the ceiling has been painted and lacquered by a pupil of Martin, who has been here for the last three years. All the small panels have paintings by Watteau; these are the

Five Senses; then two fables by Lafontaine, *Le baiser pris et rendu,* of which I had the engravings, and *Les oies de Frère Philippe.* Ah! what paintings! The frames are gilt and pierced to show the paneling. There are the Three Graces, a chimney-piece diagonally in the corner, and corner cupboards by Martin, with beautiful objects on them, including an amber desk-set which the Prince of Prussia sent him with some poems: I'll tell you about that later. The only furniture is a large armchair covered with white taffeta, and two matching stools; for, by God's grace, I haven't seen a *bergère* in the entire house.

Note that the writer gives equal weight to everyday objects as to art, to the picture frames as to the pictures, to the lacquerwork of the renowned Martin brothers as to the works of Watteau and "Veronese, etc." The reference to the lack of bergères, which were fully upholstered armchairs fashionable at the time, was meant to draw attention to the unconventional simplicity of the decor.

The owner of the *appartement* was the Marquise du Châtelet, whom Graffigny archly referred to as *la belle dame.* In fact, Émilie du Châtelet was no great beauty, but she possessed something rarer, a formidable intellect—she was an accomplished mathematician and physicist, whose translation and commentary on Isaac Newton's *Principia Mathematica* remains the standard French text to this day. She was also a talented singer and musician, a collector of books,

Louis XV bergère

diamonds, and snuffboxes, and an inveterate (though not very successful) gambler. In addition, this remarkable woman, as Nancy Mitford indelicately put it, "always had something of the whore."

The marquise's most famous romantic liaison was with the great writer Voltaire. "She understands Newton; she despises superstition and in short she makes me happy," he explained. The two were together, more or less, for fifteen years—until her death. The decoration of her country house at Cirey was one of their joint projects. Voltaire, whose business investments had made him a wealthy man, financed the work, but he didn't have the final say. "Madame du Châtelet has become architect and gardener. She is putting windows where I've put doors, she's changing staircases into chimneys, and chimneys into staircases. She's going to plant lime trees where I proposed to place elms; and if I had planted a vegetable garden, she would turn it into a flower bed," he complained. But he admired her talents. "What's more she has waved a magic wand in the house. She is able to turn rags into tapestries; she has found the secret of furnishing Cirey out of nothing."

The household arrangement at Cirey—a ménage à trois that included the marquise's complaisant husband—was unconventional. Émilie and her lover each had their own study and their own library—science hers, literature his—an astonishing 21,000 books in all.* Voltaire and Madame du Châtelet kept different hours—he worked throughout the day, she liked to work at night. While she prepared a study of Leibniz, he wrote poems, plays, and philosophical tracts. They met in the evening. Voltaire would dragoon houseguests

---

*By comparison, Jefferson's library, considered one of the largest in the new United States, consisted of about 6,500 books.

and neighbors into performing his plays in a pretty miniature theater that he had installed in the attic. Graffigny describes a midnight meal following such a performance. "After supper, Madame du Châtelet will sing an entire opera . . . We can't catch our breath here."

The lovers occupied a newly built wing next to the crumbling old chateau. The heart of their home was a gallery facing the garden. Paneled and painted yellow, it was part living room and part laboratory; in addition to the usual furniture, it housed a collection of telescopes, astronomical models, pendulums, and globes—as well as a pet parrot. The room was heated by a porcelain stove "that makes the air as warm as in the spring," wrote Graffigny. This was where the marquise played her harpsichord, and where papers and books were pushed aside to make room for morning coffee and evening supper; Graffigny describes sharing the table with an orrery. At the Château de Cirey, intellectual pursuits happily coexisted with material pleasures. One has the sense that the Enlightenment polymaths paid as much attention to decor and furnishings as to science and philosophy— they were all one.

Let's Pretend

The carving around the main entrance of Cirey was designed by Voltaire. The allegorical ornament on each side of the door—art on one side and science on the other—represented its two occupants.* The urge to decorate is as old as human history. Ornament was probably first applied to the

---

*The doorway was surmounted by a Latin quote from Virgil: "God has given us this ease."

human body, which, over the centuries, has been smeared, painted, dyed, and tattooed. Nor was this tendency limited to "primitive peoples"; Voltaire regularly wore a powdered peruke, and by all accounts whenever Émilie du Châtelet appeared in public she bedecked herself with jewels.

Ornamented tools and utensils are found in all preindustrial cultures. The decoration of utilitarian objects both humanizes them and makes them more enjoyable to use. I have a letter opener that I bought in a craft shop, made out of tornillo, a tropical hardwood. The object is as smooth as a Brancusi sculpture except for the handle, which is only partly carved; half of it is left in a natural state, the coarse grain plainly visible, a graphic reminder that this was once part of a tree. The rich dark wood—both smooth and rough—is satisfying to handle, even just to look at. Not that it slits paper any more effectively than a kitchen knife, but using this tool adds pleasure—and import—to the simple act of opening an envelope.

It is easy to forget in our functional age that, until recently, most machines and tools were ornamented, lathes as well as typewriters. Expensive shotguns are still decorated, as are some musical instruments such as harps and harpsichords, and old-fashioned implements such as fountain pens, but, on the whole, modern tools are plain. The computer on which I am writing—a Mac—has been lauded for its design, but its smooth shape is about as expressive as a toaster. Using it does not provide the same tactile and visual pleasure as my letter opener.

While few of us occupy rooms "as precious as a snuffbox," we do dress up our homes—with wallpaper, window treatments, and patterned rugs. Remove these embellishments and a house looks unlived-in. The desire to ornament can emerge in the least likely circumstances. I've seen mud huts in African villages whose front doors were carefully outlined with colored paint. The modest decoration was prompted by the same impulse that makes Americans decorate their front doors for Thanksgiving and Christmas: celebrating entry into the home.

The British architectural historian John Summerson pointed out that there are two distinct types of ornament. One simply modulates surfaces with patterns or decorative designs. Surface modulation provides a focus for the eye, as well as a contrast between surfaces that are ornamented and surfaces that are plain. It can also provide a tactile experience, a sense of scale, a definition of edges, or the articulation of different parts. In a Louis XV armchair, for example, the floral pattern on the upholstery fabric can mimic the carved motifs on the legs and arms.

The second type of ornament Summerson called "subjunctive" (he admitted it was an awkward term). What he meant was the desire to make something appear "as if" it were other than it really was: a rosette carved out of wood, a plant motif embroidered on a chairback, or a guilloche chain carved on a chair rail. Subjunctive ornament can be natural forms rendered in inert materials, or forms transposed from one material to another. A rococo chair may have arms carved like foliage, and feet in the shape of clenched animal claws. Such ornament brings to mind the frisson of wonder at an illusionist's levitation or a conjurer's card trick. The world is not what it appears to be.

Subjunctive ornament could be called "let's pretend," since play is never far beneath the surface. Because we have learned to treat classical architecture with a respect that often borders on reverence, it is easy to miss how joyful and even prankish classical ornament can be. Although plants carried serious symbolic meanings in the ancient world—

the evergreen stood for eternity, the vine for fertility, the oak for wisdom—the rotund fruits, curling leaves, and sinuous stalks also introduce a frolicsome quality that undermines the solidity of architecture. A seventeenth-century British visitor to Venice described a Corinthian capital, which is a riot of acanthus leaves that resembles tumbled hair, as "decked like a wanton courtesan."

Garlands, fronds, swags, and other floral motifs, whether carved in wood or cast in bronze, turn eighteenth-century armchairs into horticultural samplers. A profusion of encrusted shells and sea urchins gives the impression of something pulled from the briny deep. When tastes shifted to the neoclassical, furniture legs resembled fluted columns and marquetry was more likely to show classical ruins than floral arrangements.

Whatever its iconographic or symbolic content, ornament inevitably blurs the distinction between what we perceive with our senses and what we intellectually know to be true. That is why ornament has always consisted of plant life, chains, ropes, and knots, as well as human and animal figures. Such decoration starts by catching the eye, and ends by engaging the mind. As Voltaire famously quipped about luxury: "The superfluous is such a necessary thing!"

Art and Function

I own an eighteenth-century French snuffbox, a family heirloom, but I don't have a rococo chair. Not that I could afford one—a gilded Louis XV armchair, originally commissioned by Madame de Pompadour, sold at Sotheby's in 2013 for $653,000. In any case, a rococo chair would look out of place in our home, which is austere by ancien régime standards.

However, I do have a pair of beautiful chairs that similarly combine art with function. They are fully upholstered armchairs, modern versions of a bergère. The plump upholstery swells lasciviously, like Madame de Pompadour's bodice, and the gently curved legs are tapered, giving the impression of a ballerina *en pointe*. The upholstery material has a copper-colored thread running through it that creates an eye-catching glimmer as well as a pleasing geometrical pattern. The chairs have a languorous sense of luxury. It's hard to pinpoint exactly why. It has something to do with the generous proportions, the sensuous curves of the upholstery, and the shapely saber legs. The other chairs in my living room appear dowdy compared with this pair of glamorous beauties.

The beauties are the work of John Dunnigan, a contemporary Rhode Island furniture maker whose work is sometimes called "studio furniture." Like eighteenth-century cabinetwork, studio furniture is produced one piece at a time. Moreover, like his earlier counterpart, the studio furniture maker is able to shape wood, finish surfaces, and stretch fabrics in ways that are either impossible or impractical in a factory or on an assembly line. Making furniture the old-fashioned way provides opportunities for personal expression which, in Dunnigan's case, is sometimes mischievous. "One of the best things about rules is figuring out how to break them," he says. The rule that my chairs break is the rule of symmetry. The curved backs, which resemble lotus leaves, are asymmetrical, each chair a mirror of its mate, which makes them appear to be leaning toward each other—as if they were separated at birth. They are definitely a pair.

American studio furniture originated in the 1950s. What distinguished woodworkers such as Wharton Esherick, George Nakashima, and Sam Maloof from other furniture

Conoid Chair
(George Nakashima)

designers was their firm rejection of mass production (they built the furniture themselves, by hand) as well as their use of preindustrial materials (they worked exclusively in wood). The handcrafted furniture movement of the 1950s is sometimes called a revival, but it was a revival of skills, not of forms. This plain and undecorated furniture, although often inspired by early American folk models, resembles the abstract sculptures of Henry Moore and Jean Arp, a curious mixture of preindustrial craft and modernist aesthetics.

Dunnigan belongs to the second generation of studio furniture makers, which emerged in the 1980s. Some of these craftsmen moved from utility to artistic expression, creating fanciful chairs that are more like sculpture than furniture. Others accepted the traditional discipline of furniture-making, combining utility with beauty. Dunnigan belongs to the second group—his chairs not only look like chairs, they are often versions of specific types of chairs: armchairs, slipper chairs, side chairs, sofas. Versions, but not imitations. The exaggerated wedge-shaped seats of my chairs, for example, create the impression of forced perspective so that the chairs seem to be opening up to receive the sitter, and owe something to eighteenth-century cabriole chairs. The faceted saber legs, on the other hand, recall the klismos, while the plump asymmetry and the contrasting textures of bubinga wood and cotton damask veer away from historical precedent. Every time I walk through the living room, I can't help running my hand over the curved back. What does that

Pair of armchairs
(John Dunnigan)

tactile experience of a chair have to do with sitting? Nothing—
and everything.

What about comfort? "There is a necessary distinction to
be made between trying to design something that is comfortable," Dunnigan once wrote, "and trying to design something that is not uncomfortable." Defining sitting comfort is
like trying to prove a negative, because it is often discomfort
that is more immediately experienced when sitting in a poorly
designed chair. This may be soreness of the thighs if the front
edge of the seat is too high, or stiffness of the neck if the
angle of the chairback causes the head to be out of alignment
with the spine. The most common discomfort is felt when a
chair is too hard, which causes stresses in the muscles and
tissues of the body.

My Dunnigan chairs are extremely comfortable. Both my
wife and I, despite a difference in body size (I am larger), find
the chairs equally accommodating. For all their resemblance
to a French bergère these are not easy chairs. Dunnigan says
that he wanted to replicate the calm position of someone
meditating—back straight, arms at rest. "I wanted a person
to be able to sit without noticing the chair." The sitting position in my chair is upright rather than slouched, so the head,
neck, and spine are aligned; the arms are slightly lower than
usual, so the shoulders are relaxed. The exact form of the

chair is the result of trial and error; Dunnigan built a number of fully upholstered mock-ups before he finalized the dimensions.

The sprung upholstery of my chairs has a lot to do with their comfort. Sprung upholstery appeared in the nineteenth century and is not normally associated with modern designer furniture, which tends to rely on foam and thin padding. The presence of sprung upholstery in Dunnigan's chairs is a reminder that truly comfortable sitting furniture is difficult to achieve without carefully considered upholstery, and that a good chair provides support for the body as well as pleasure for the eye.

Dunnigan has given a lot of thought to the art of furniture-making.

> If I had to describe my furniture, I would say that it's sensual sometimes, that it's comfortable sometimes, that it's traditional or historically referenced sometimes, but it's really about what I see as a basic issue of human existence—it's about how a person moves their body in space and how they interact with other objects. Furniture is about how the body sits on it or puts something on it. It would be the same for someone living in 2000 A.D. or 2000 B.C.

This is an important insight. Yes, a chair is an everyday object—even if it's sometimes decorated—but it's an everyday object with which the human body has an intimate relationship. You sit down in an armchair and it embraces you, you rub against it, you caress the fabric, touch the wood, grip the arms. It is this intimacy, not merely utility, that ultimately distinguishes a beautiful chair from a beautiful painting. If you sit on it, can it still be art? Perhaps it is more.

THREE

Sitting Up

There is a pivotal early scene in David Lean's film *Lawrence of Arabia* in which T. E. Lawrence and his superior, Colonel Brighton, visit the desert encampment of Prince Faisal, a leader of the Arab Revolt. The royal tent is spartan yet luxurious, patterned woven cloths hang from the low ceiling, a large brass samovar gleams in the candlelight, the ground is covered with a rich carpet. There is no furniture; the men sit on the carpet. Brighton in his tailored uniform, polished Sam Browne belt, and riding boots looks distinctly ill at ease with his legs awkwardly stretched out in front of him. Lawrence, a lieutenant and less formally dressed, appears slightly more comfortable, with his legs folded to one side. The prince, attired in a dark robe and a white *ghutrah*, reclines on a pile of sheepskins, while his colleague, Sherif Ali, leans casually against a tent pole. The various postures cinematically underline a central point: the relaxed Bedouins are at home in this place—the desert—while the stiff English colonel is an interloper. Lawrence is somewhere in between.

The world is divided into people who sit on the floor and those who sit on chairs. In a classic study of human posture

around the world, the anthropologist Gordon W. Hewes identified no fewer than one hundred common sitting positions.
"At least a fourth of mankind habitually takes the load off
its feet by crouching in a deep squat, both at rest and at work,"
he observed. Deep squatting is favored by people in Southeast Asia, Africa, and Latin America, but sitting cross-legged
on the floor is almost as common. Many South Asians cook,
dine, work, and relax in that position. Sedentary kneeling,
that is, sitting on the heels with the knees on the floor, is
practiced by Japanese, Koreans, and Eurasians, and also used
by Muslims at prayer. The half-kneeling position, one knee
up and one down, that I saw in ancient Egyptian paintings
occurs among Australian aborigines, some native Americans, and black Africans; a variant in the American West is
known as the "cowboy squat." Certain Native American
tribes in the Southwest, as well as Melanesians, customar-
ily sit on the floor with legs stretched straight out or crossed
at the ankles. Sitting with the legs folded to one side—
Lawrence's position above—is described by Hewes as a pre-
dominantly female posture in many tribal societies.

The diversity of different postures around the world could
be caused by differences in climate, dress, or lifestyle. Cold
or damp floors would discourage kneeling and squatting
and might lead people to seek raised alternatives; tight clothing would tend to inhibit deep squatting and cross-legged
sitting; nomadic peoples would be less likely to use furniture
than urban societies; and so on. But cause-and-effect does
not explain why folding stools originated in ancient Egypt,
a region with a warm, dry climate. Or why the Japanese and
Koreans, who have cold winters, both traditionally sat on
floor mats. Or why the nomadic Mongols traveled with
collapsible furniture, while the equally nomadic Bedouins
did not.

Hewes explained that he did not include the reclining position in his research because he did not find sufficient photographic evidence. That is a shame because reclining has always been a comfortable position for the body at rest. The ancient Egyptians used beds, and may have reclined on couches, although these do not appear in wall paintings—banquet scenes show people on chairs, or sitting on the ground. The earliest pictorial evidence of dining in a reclined position is a seventh-century B.C. bas-relief in the British Museum. The alabaster carving sometimes called *The Garden Party* shows an Assyrian king and his wife being served food and drink outdoors—they are celebrating a victorious battle. The king is reclining on a couch that resembles a chaise longue, while the queen is seated nearby in an armchair; they share a table laden with food. What is unusual about the furniture is that it is very tall: the couch is about five feet off the ground, and the queen's armchair, which reminds me of a lifeguard's chair, is waist-high and requires a footstool. The reason for this height is to elevate the sitters above the servants, who wield fly whisks with handles as long as broomsticks to fan the royal couple. A ghoulish detail: the head of the king's vanquished enemy hangs from a nearby tree.

Homer describes diners seated at tables, but by the sixth century B.C. the dining couch had arrived in Greece, probably from Mesopotamia. By all accounts Greek homes were sparsely furnished, and dining couches were used as chaises longues during the day and beds at night—all uses are depicted on Greek pottery. Couches were generally elevated, with iron, bronze, or wood frames, the mattress resting on leather or cord lacings. Although the Greeks used stools and chairs, they must have spent much time socializing in a reclined position.

Like so many Greek customs, the reclining posture

migrated to Rome. The Met has an example of a Roman couch (reconstructed from fragments recovered at an imperial villa) dating from the first or second century A.D. Raised at each end, the couch resembles a recamier, except that the Roman idea of status required that it be elevated; it is the height of a modern kitchen counter and is mounted with the aid of a footstool. Couches were used for informal conversation, for resting, and also for dining. The arrangement in a dining room, or triclinium (literally, three couches), consisted of three wide couches, each holding three occupants, placed on three sides of a large square table (the fourth side left open to allow the servants access). The diners—only men used the triclinium—leaned on their left elbows in a semirecumbent position, serving themselves with their right hands.

The Austrian architect Bernard Rudofsky is best remembered for a series of provocative books, including *Architecture Without Architects*, based on a 1964 exhibition at the Museum of Modern Art, where he was a curator. Something of a design gadfly, he applauded the custom of prone dining. He observed that Roman diners, with but one hand free, had no use for cutlery, thus doing away with what he called table clutter. A cheerful iconoclast, Rudofsky despised the functional modern bathroom, for example, and disliked most domestic labor-saving devices. He particularly ridi-

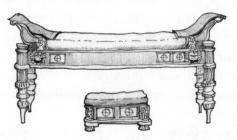

Roman couch

culed chairs. "The more sensitive among us are aware of the ludicrous aspects of sitting on chairs—impaled on four toothpicks, as it were, or, draped limp like an oyster, over what resembles an outsized halfshell."

Rudofsky's rather strained description was a calculated challenge to those who considered chair-sitting to be culturally superior to floor-sitting. He was certainly correct that the lack of chairs is not a sign of either primitiveness or ignorance. The refined Japanese and Koreans were long aware of sitting furniture, but chose to sit on floor mats instead. In India, upright sitting was introduced more than two centuries ago by the British, yet most people still perform a variety of tasks—cooking, eating, working—while seated cross-legged on the floor.

Selecting one sitting posture over another has far-reaching consequences. If you sit on floor mats, you are likely to develop an etiquette that requires removing footwear before entering the home. You are also more likely to wear sandals or slippers rather than laced-up shoes, and loose clothing that enables you to squat or sit cross-legged. Floor-sitters tend not to use tall wardrobes—it is more convenient to store things in chests and low cabinets closer to floor level. People who sit on mats are more likely to sleep on mats, too, just as chair-sitters are more likely to sleep in beds.* Chair-sitting societies develop a variety of furniture such as dining tables, dressing tables, coffee tables, desks, and sideboards. Sitting on the floor also affects architecture: walking around the house in bare feet or socks demands smooth floors—no splinters—preferably warm wood rather than stone; places to sit are likely to be covered with soft mats or woven carpets; tall windowsills and very tall ceilings hold less appeal.

---

*India, where many people who sit on the floor use beds, is an exception.

Lastly, posture has direct physical effects. A lifetime of sitting unsupported on the floor develops muscles not required for chair-sitting, which is why chair-sitters, unaccustomed to sitting cross-legged, soon become uncomfortable in that position. And vice versa. People in India regularly sit up on train seats and waiting-room benches in the cross-legged position, which they find more comfortable than sitting with feet hanging down.

The ancient Egyptians were unusual in combining floor-sitting and chair-sitting, but in general the two customs make awkward partners. A chair in a room of floor-sitters is a rude intruder. Conversely, sitting on the floor among chairs is socially acceptable only when there is no other place to sit—and then only under certain circumstances such as in a crowded auditorium or airport waiting room. Sitting on the floor among chair-sitters disrupts the order of things, which is probably why teenagers like to do it. For precisely the same reason, sitting on the floor was fashionable among the European avant-garde in the 1920s, among the Beats in the 1950s, and among student protestors in the 1960s—it upset convention.

The Barbarian Bed

For thousands of years, the ancient Chinese sat and slept on the floor. But at the beginning of the second century A.D. this changed; they adopted the folding stool, and eventually the full range of sitting furniture. Why and how this happened tells us a lot about the social and cultural functions of chairs. The stage for this momentous change was set in northern China and Manchuria. Because this region has severe winters, sitting and sleeping on cold floors is uncomfortable and unhealthy, and as a result the northern Chinese invented an unusual device. The *kang* was a brick platform warmed by heated air passing through underfloor flues. Raised about two feet off the floor and covered in felt pads, woven mats, or rugs, the *kang* typically extended across the full width of the room and served as a sleeping platform. During the day, sleeping quilts were folded and placed on the side, and the raised area served—and still serves in some rural households—as the main living space of the home.

During the summer the Chinese slept on beds. Beds appeared very early in China: a bed has been found in a burial site that dates from the third or fourth century B.C. A second-century B.C. tomb painting shows men seated cross-legged on a bed, suggesting that beds were also used as divans. Eventually, beds were fitted with low railings on three sides, and a folded sleeping quilt provided a padded backrest, creating a sort of couch. Thus, from very early times, the Chinese were distinguished from other East Asian cultures by combining sitting on the floor with sitting up, not on chairs but on raised furniture.

This pragmatism may explain the apparent ease with which, in the second century A.D., the Chinese adopted the stool. Here is an ancient description: "The [stool] has movable joints so that its legs can be crossed. It is threaded with cords to make it comfortable to sit upon. It can be folded in a moment. It only weighs a few catties [a few pounds]." This obviously describes an X-frame folding stool, identical to the type used by the Egyptians and later by the Minoans and the Greeks. The Chinese called the stool *hu chuang*. *Hu* (barbarian) was how they referred to anything foreign, and because there was no word for chair or stool they used *chuang* (bed), which was the only piece of sitting furniture they knew. The barbarian bed was evidently a cultural import, but from

where? None of China's immediate neighbors used stools, so the
source must have been farther away.
Caravan routes linked northern
China across the Gobi Desert and
Persia to the Mediterranean port
cities of Alexandria and Antioch.
Hence, the most likely source for the
hu chuang was the eastern reaches of
the Roman Empire, precisely the area
where the folding stool originated.

Chinese folding stool

Chinese folding stools were sometimes used as portable
garden seats, and as camp furniture by military officers;
where stools were *never* used was in the home. Just as modern-
day Americans might spread a blanket on the ground for a
picnic, but would not think of doing so in their living rooms,
the ancient Chinese could not imagine bringing the *hu
chuang* indoors. In the home, one sat on floor mats.

For several hundred years, the two different sitting
postures—cross-legged on floor mats, and legs-down on
stools—coexisted. It was not until the tenth century that the
chair appeared. The stage was set sometime in the second or
third century A.D. when, having acquired the habit of sitting
on the raised *kang*—and on bed-couches—the Chinese created a portable *kang* in the form of a wooden platform. The
wooden *kang*—the name was the same—was supported by
a carved open frame and came in a variety of sizes, large
enough to accommodate several sitters or small enough for
a single person.* The light platform could be easily moved

---

*The brick *kang* and the wooden *kang* have a similar-sounding name but are
written differently. The ideograph for the former signifies "fire," while that for
the latter signifies "box."

from room to room or into the garden. People sat on it cross-legged, as they did on a stone *kang*. These movable daises accommodated a wide variety of activities—eating, studying, playing board games, relaxing.

Platform living spread throughout China during the Tang dynasty, a period when the country was reunified and people and ideas moved freely from north to south. A Tang mural shows a group of scholars at a banquet, sitting on wooden platforms arranged on three sides of a low table laden with dishes. The platforms and the table are both about knee-height. Most of the diners sit cross-legged, but two or three of them have one foot dangling over the edge. Sooner or later, the second foot will come down, and the dais will become—a seat.

A traditional stone *kang* allowed sitters to lean comfortably against the wall (just as an outdoor sitter leans back against a tree), but a freestanding wooden platform offered no such convenience. At some point, someone had the idea of adding a back to the platform. Once sitters were able to lean against a back, and also sit on the edge with the feet down, it did not take a great leap of the imagination to turn the wooden *kang* into a chair.

The decisive shift from floor-sitting to chair-sitting occurred during the Song dynasty. Frame chairs, with and without arms, are illustrated in scroll paintings of the tenth century. The oldest surviving Chinese chair, excavated by archaeologists in 1920, is a side chair dating from the eleventh century. It is called a yokeback chair because the curved top rail extends at each end and resembles the yoke of an oxcart. The sophisticated design uses mortise-and-tenon joints, stretchers to reinforce the legs, and a woven cane seat. Most important, it also includes an S-shaped splat to support the lumbar region of the back—the oldest known use of this device in the history of the chair. The yokeback—with and without arms—remained unchanged for centuries, and became the standard Chinese chair, used in reception rooms, banqueting halls, studies, and bedrooms. Being light, it was easily moved and could be carried outside. Upholstery was unknown although loose cushions were used, and for special occasions a colorful embroidered silk runner was draped over the yoke and the seat. The Chinese

Song dynasty yokeback chair

named their homegrown chair *yi*, which is derived from the verb "to lean"—one sat on a stool, but one leaned back on a chair.

Tenth-century China is the unique case of a premodern floor-sitting culture that adopted the chair voluntarily, rather than as the result of conquest or colonization. The societal change was dramatic and swift. A copy of a tenth-century scroll painting, *The Night Revels of Han Xizai*, shows a banquet in the home of Han Xizai, a scholar and court dignitary. A woman playing a Chinese lute is entertaining the group; she is seated on a stool. Three male visitors occupy yokeback chairs. Han and a friend are seated on a wooden *kang* with a backrest on three sides. Several guests are standing but no one is sitting on the floor; indeed, there are no floor mats. Food and drinks are laid out on small tables. What is remarkable is the variety of sitting postures. Two of the chair-sitters are upright, the third leans forward, listening intently to the music, his hands on his knees—a very modern position. On the other hand, both Han and his friend sit on the platform in traditional floor-sitting postures: Han is cross-legged, while his friend, more casual, leans against the back-rest with one knee raised. This scene exemplifies the Chinese culture's ability to mix innovation and tradition.

This mixture lasted a long time. A French diplomat recounted a visit to Peking in 1795. "The mandarins had assumed that we would sit cross-legged on the floor," he recorded. "But seeing that we found this posture very un-comfortable, they took us into a great pavilion . . . furnished with tables and chairs." The Frenchman described the furni-ture as arranged on a platform, which had "a thick carpet and they lit a fire underneath." In other words, the furniture was placed on top of a heated *kang*.

A domestic revolution accompanied the adoption of the chair in China. Women started wearing trousers; people no longer removed their shoes before entering the home, and the outdoor veranda, which previously had served as a place to leave one's footwear, lost this function. Waist-high dining tables, desks, gaming tables, and worktables appeared. So did tall lamps and washstands, as well as cheval mirrors. The dimensions of rooms changed to accommodate these objects; ceilings became taller. These innovations arrived in grand homes first, but soon spread to modest dwellings, for chairs were used by all strata of Chinese society; Song dynasty paintings show chairs and stools being used by common folk in roadside inns. When the Emperor Huizong commissioned his official portrait, he chose to sit not on an elaborate throne but on a yokeback side chair. The chair, which is finished in red lacquer and has an embroidered silk throw, is tall enough to require a footstool.

What were the conditions in China that facilitated the adoption of such a radically new form of furniture? Accord-ing to the French historian Fernand Braudel, changes in the furnishings have always been constrained by two conditions.

First, poverty. "Interiors change hardly at all in the world of the poor," he wrote. Floor-sitting required only mats and cushions, whereas chairs—and the furniture that accompanied chair-sitting—were expensive. Such a shift required prosperity. "Rule number two: traditional civilizations remain faithful to their accustomed decor." That is why the age-old sitting postures that Gordon Hewes documented—among aborigines, pastoral people, and remote tribes—have hardly changed in centuries.

Tenth-century China was a period of not only prosperity but also intense social upheaval. Improved rice production led to dramatic population growth; maritime trade developed with India, Africa, and the Muslim world; the economy was further stimulated by the introduction of paper money (for the first time anywhere in the world). Public affairs were administered by a newly formed civil bureaucracy. Moreover, this period was remarkably inventive, producing movable-type printing, astronomical clocks, and gunpowder. Living in the midst of such momentous change, it is little wonder that people were open to seeing the world from a different vantage point: up on a chair.

"Chair-sitting and furniture, possibly the chief distinguishing postural attribute of Western civilization, go hand in hand," Hewes observed, "though it is difficult to tell which is cause and which effect, whether the habit of sitting on a support led to the invention of stools, benches and chairs or vice versa." In China, at least, the habit of sitting up seems to have arrived first. The imported folding stool did not cause people to abandon sitting on mats and wooden platforms. Rather, it was the habit of leaning back, and of sitting with the feet lowered, that prepared the way for the adoption of the chair.

Chinese Household Furniture, published in 1948, was only the second book in English on the subject, and the first to enjoy wide circulation. Its author, George Norbert Kates, was an American scholar who lived in Peking for seven years immediately prior to World War II and experienced what he called the "Old China." His summary of the evolution of sitting habits, while based on the fragmentary and partial evidence available to him at the time, still rings true:

> It appears possible that as civilization progressed in China, men sat ever farther away from the ground; first directly upon it, no doubt, then later upon mats, as we can see in familiar arrangements in paintings where the sages of old are represented. Those of rank were placed upon low, broad wooden platforms, also provided with matting, and these seem gradually to have developed until they finally become true couches. Many later pictures show examples of them being used by personages of honor, while next to them sit secondary figures in armchairs, themselves attended by still others a little lower on stools.

There were many Chinese stools: folding stools, four-legged wooden stools, round stools, and drumlike porcelain stools. Chinese stools could be utilitarian but they could also be luxurious, beautifully carved hardwood with inset seats of woven cane or palm fiber. Such stools were considered particularly appropriate for ladies. Stools were used in ways different from the West: they sometimes served as low tables, and they were commonly taken out of doors.

Kates observed that although chairs were sometimes provided for special guests, or for the elderly, diners normally sat on stools. This practice dated back to the tenth century. In a painting attributed to Emperor Huizong and showing a small outdoor banquet, the guests are seated on wooden drum stools around a large square table resembling a platform. Sitting at a table coincided with a change in how and what people ate. When China had been a mat-sitting culture, food was served on low individual tables—resembling modern bed trays—that were brought from the kitchen already laden. Now people sat around a large table, leaning forward to serve themselves from platters, sharing in a communal experience. It is surely no coincidence that the custom of eating together, serving oneself from common dishes, seated around a table on stools, emerged during the Song dynasty concurrently with what many consider the world's first great national cuisine.

Prosperity and cultural change are prerequisites for the adoption of new social customs, but they are not sufficient causes. Cultures pick and choose. The Japanese meticulously copied many Chinese artifacts and practices, including architecture, calligraphy, art, and dress, as well as sitting on mats. But they ignored the folding stool and the wooden platform, and although they periodically flirted with chair-sitting, the fashion never caught on and Japanese life remained at floor level.* Conversely, while the Greeks copied much of their furniture from the Egyptians, they did not sit on the floor; indeed, they considered people who squatted to be uncivilized, perhaps because their old enemies, the Persians, sat on cushions and divans. During the Renaissance, Italians copied Roman architecture and admired Roman art, but they never adopted the Roman habit of reclined dining. On the other hand, in Spain, where Islamic fashions persisted long after the Moorish occupation ended, according to Braudel, as late as the seventeenth century it was still the custom for elegant la-

---

*Modern Japanese homes have Western-style (yōshitsu) rooms with sitting furniture, but they also often include a separate washitsu, or traditional room, with tatami mats for sitting on the floor.

dies at court to sit on floor cushions. The willingness to alter or abandon—or not abandon—a long-standing custom is never predetermined. Ultimately, cultures choose to sit up or down because they want to.

The Sitting Position

Any culture that decides to sit on chairs must come to terms with a challenging reality: human posture. The first person to recognize the connection between sitting and posture was the eighteenth-century French physician Nicolas Andry de Boisregard. Andry was a pioneer in the field of orthopedics—he coined the term—and in his 1741 treatise he described the connection between healthy sitting posture and chairs. "When one sits with the body bended backwards, the back must necessarily be crooked inwards," he wrote, "and when one sits upon a hollow seat, the effort which one naturally makes, and without any design, to bring the body to an equilibrium, must of necessity make the back still more crooked." The hollow seat referred to the concave woven rush seats of ordinary chairs, which tended to sag over time. To improve posture, Andry proposed adding an adjustable screw that would push up on the seat from beneath, keeping it flat.

Two hundred years after Andry, Ellen Davis Kelly, a physical education professor at the University of Oklahoma, neatly summarized the physiological challenge of human posture in a teaching handbook:

Posture is a distinct problem to humans because the skeleton is fundamentally unstable in the upright position. A four or even a three-legged chair or stool can be quite stable. But who ever heard of a two-legged

piece of furniture? The two-legged human body pres-
ents a continuous problem in maintaining balance, a
problem augmented because the feet are a very small
base of support for a towering superstructure. And
as though this were not problem enough, the trunk,
head, and arms are supported from the hips upward
by a one-legged arrangement of the spine.

The purpose of the chair is to provide respite from this
precarious balancing act. But the instability that Kelly describes is, if anything, compounded when one sits down. The
weight of the body is concentrated on the ischial tuberosities,
or sitting bones, at the base of the pelvis. These bones, which
resemble the rockers of a rocking chair, provide support
only laterally and allow the body to rock back and forth in
the other direction. A chairback provides the support that allows the muscles to relax, but a too-vertical backrest causes
the sitter to slump, while simply angling the seatback creates
an unnatural backward leaning posture. If the seat is too
hard, it will cause discomfort to the sitting bones, and if it is
too soft it will distort the buttock muscles and will press
on the ischia, likewise causing discomfort. If a chair is too
low, the body's weight will all be concentrated on the sitting
bones instead of being carried by the thighs; if a chair is too
high, the sitter will tend to slump forward to place the feet in
a more stable position on the floor, but this will constrict
breathing and create muscle tension in the neck.

In 1884, a German orthopedic surgeon, Franz Staffel,
judging that most chairs were "constructed more for the eye
than for the back," proposed a low backrest that supported
the lumbar region. Staffel, who has been called "the father
of the modern school chair," recommended that when sitting, the back should approximate as closely as possible the

double-S curve of the spine when standing upright. During the nineteenth century, when primary education became obligatory and children spent more and more time sitting in the classroom, researchers proposed a variety of chair-desk combinations intended to improve posture. Some of the designs included seat belts, forehead restraints, and face rests, although it is hard to imagine that such draconian devices were ever actually used.

In 1913, a Swiss anatomist, Hans Strasser, published the design of a chair whose upper backrest was slightly angled, and whose seat was sloped to better support the underside of the thighs. Strasser's findings were confirmed thirty-five years later by Bengt Åkerblom, a Swedish researcher, who used X-rays and electromyograms to study the body mechanics of sitting. Åkerblom designed several chairs whose bent backrest became known as the "Åkerblom curve."

The movement of standing up and sitting down is also a challenge. We have all experienced the rude jolt when we miscalculate the height of a chair, because dropping into a chair briefly exerts twice our body weight on the spine. The design solution to this problem is the armrest, which provides something to hold on to as we lower ourselves into the seat and is also a handy place to push up from as we rise. This is especially important if a chair is low, like a lounge chair.* Getting up from a low chair without arms can be difficult,

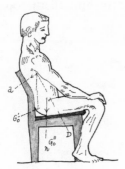

Chair with lumbar support (after Hans Strasser)

---

*A lounge chair can be as low as fourteen inches, compared with eighteen inches for a typical side chair.

especially for the elderly. Armrests serve another purpose: relieving some of the stress from the shoulders by providing something on which to lean while we are sitting.

The British psychologist Paul Branton described the seated body as "not merely an inert bag of bones, dumped for a time in a seat, but a live organism in a dynamic state of continuous activity." We don't sit still—we fidget, we shift our weight, even if ever so slightly, crossing our legs and arms, moving our cramped muscles. We interact with our chairs: we sit on them, lean back and lean forward, and often perch on the edge of our seats. We wrap our leg around our chair's leg; we sling one arm across its back, or a leg across its arm.

We are good at walking and running, and we are happy lying down when we sleep. It is the in-between position that is the problem. This is true even if we sit on the ground—as attested by the variety of pads, bolsters, armrests, and cushions used by floor-sitting cultures. It is even truer when we choose to sit on a chair. Every chair represents a struggle to resolve the conflict between gravity and the human anatomy. Sitting up is always a challenge.

FOUR

A Chair on the Side

A side chair is a straight-backed chair without arms. Like a side issue or a side dish it is of lower rank. An armchair bestows a certain stature, you sit *in* it; a side chair is more prosaic—you sit *on* it, whether you are attending a social function, eating a sandwich, or simply tying your shoelaces. My oldest side chair, one of a pair bought years ago in a roadside flea market, is a straightforward affair. The seat is a slab of solid wood with carved depressions shaped to fit the buttocks and a slight slope so that you slide back against the wooden spindles and the curved top rail. The chair feels stable; the four slightly splayed legs are countersunk into the seat and braced with dowel-like stretchers. Homely and unsophisticated though it may be, this kitchen chair gives me pleasure every time I sit on it. It's like using a claw hammer or a crosscut saw, or indeed any tool that has been refined over centuries—it feels right.

Side chairs have been around a lot longer than claw hammers.* The oldest representation of a chair that I came across

---

*The claw hammer, like the forged iron nail, was invented by the ancient Romans.

during my visit to the Metropolitan Museum was in a gallery devoted to Cycladic, Minoan, and Mycenaean art. The Cyclades are a group of islands in the southwestern Aegean Sea that was settled in the Late Neolithic period, probably by people from Asia Minor. The island chain was home to a prosperous farming and maritime trading society that predated the Minoan culture by several centuries. The chief surviving records of this prehistoric culture are hundreds of figurines whose function remains obscure; they may have been cult images, protective talismans, or funerary accessories (most have been found in grave sites). It was one of these that caught my eye.

The sculpture was about twelve inches tall. Carved in white marble, it depicted a seated man playing a harp. The harpist, who had an elongated stylized face that anticipated Brancusi, was plucking his instrument with his thumb. His head was thrown back, and he appeared to be singing. It was his chair that interested me: an ordinary side chair with four straight legs without stretchers, and a slightly sloping back. The sole distinctive feature was the backrest, which had a curved top rail and an oval insert—the world's first medallion chair? Cycladic chairs were most likely made of wood—the tenons connecting the legs to the seat rail are plainly visible in the sculpture. The seat was probably woven cord or plaited rushes.

The label in the glass case informed me that the sculpture dated from 2800–2700 B.C. I was bowled over. I had spent the day looking at examples of Egyptian chairs, most of which were thronelike and cere-

Cycladic harpist
sculpture

monial. Yet a thousand years earlier, the inhabitants of a small island in the Aegean were making ordinary side chairs. There are Cycladic figurines of musicians sitting on four-legged stools as well as chairs, and it is obvious that this was a chair-sitting culture. Unfortunately, so little is known of this society, which left no written records, that how and why they became sitters remains a mystery.

Around 2000 B.C., the Cycladic civilization was absorbed by its larger Minoan neighbor. Historians surmise that the Minoans used beds, couches, and sitting furniture, although the surviving evidence is scant, with the notable exception of the Knossos camp stool, which was likely copied from the Egyptians. The Greeks adopted the folding stool, too, and their thronelike armchairs were based on Egyptian and Western Asiatic models.

There is one original Greek contribution to the history of the chair: the klismos. This chair was distinguished by its curved saber legs and a broad curved backrest at roughly shoulder height. The rear legs were continuous S-shaped pieces, and the front legs were similarly curved. The seat was a loose cushion supported by leather thongs. The delicately tapered and curved saber legs (there were no stretchers) give the chair an instantly recognizable profile that appears in many ancient bas-reliefs and vase paintings.

Klismos chair

Where did the klismos come from? It was neither a replica nor a variant, in the Kubleresque sense; it was something much rarer: an original. The klismos appeared in Greece in the middle of the fifth century B.C., seemingly out of the blue; it had no Egyptian or Assyrian antecedents, nor was it based on earlier Greek models. Like the Greek temple, once the klismos achieved its essential form, it remained virtually unchanged for hundreds of years—arms were never added.

The ancient Greeks copied couches, armchairs, and folding stools from other cultures, so what compelled them to invent this beautifully proportioned chair? In a word, posture. The Greeks favored a relaxed posture—hence the popularity of couches—and the klismos, which had a slightly reclined back, allowed the sitter to slouch; in that sense, it was more like a lounge chair. On the other hand, the saber legs were pure fancy—difficult to fabricate and structurally challenging, they could easily crack if they were too slender (it is noteworthy that Greek armchairs, couches, and stools had straight legs). The klismos was an easeful chair, but surely it was not simply the desire for comfort that impelled its design. Maybe it was a result of the Greeks' need for beauty, the same need that made them lavish so much attention on their temples. Or should one look to Greek humanist ideals? Illustrations of klismos chairs show a variety of occupants: gods and heroes, philosophers and poets, musicians and potters, men and women. This was not a throne or a ceremonial chair. Rather it was a chair for everyday use—by everyone. A democratic chair.

The klismos is considered by many to be the most graceful chair ever made. During the Greek Revival of the late eighteenth century, the design was copied by cabinetmakers in Scandinavia, France, Britain, and the United States. The American architect Benjamin Latrobe designed several klismos-inspired chairs, including a set for the oval drawing room of the White House. Architects in particular were drawn to the klismos: Karl Friedrich Schinkel designed a version; so did Erik Gunnar Asplund and Josef Frank; and the saber legs of the klismos undoubtedly influenced Mies van der Rohe's Barcelona Chair. It is not possible to test an ancient klismos, because no original Greek chairs have survived, but I had the opportunity to try a recent version: an inexpensive chair designed by the architect Michael Graves for JCPenney. This chair is made of rubberwood, a plantation hardwood from Southeast Asia, and has a padded seat and stretchers to reinforce the legs, but the characteristic curved backrest and saber legs are unmistakable. As I expected, it was comfortable.

Like the folding stool, the klismos is a sitting tool distilled to its essence. But it is also a cultural artifact of great aesthetic refinement. You can copy it, as the British cabinetmaker Thomas Hope did. You can decorate it, as Latrobe did—although that does not really make it a better chair. Or you can figure out how to mass-produce it, as Graves did. But you can't really improve it. It's perfect.

Reincarnation

The curule chair was based on the Greek folding stool, but the Romans showed no interest in the klismos. The few representations of the chair in Roman art are simply copies of Greek originals. The Romans did use thronelike armchairs, as well as wicker chairs that resemble modern tub chairs, but the most common seat was the stool. Roman stools could be plain or elaborate, with four legs or with a curved X-frame like a curule chair. Variations included a settee-type stool for two, and an elongated stool—that is, a bench. Stools and benches were utilitarian, which probably appealed to the practical Romans.

With the fall of the empire, Roman furniture, like so many

other artifacts—public baths, aqueducts, paved roads—was forgotten. So was the custom of reclining at the dining table. At a medieval table, the head of the household might occupy a heavy armchair—the "great chair"—but the rest of the diners sat on benches, which were the standard form of table seating. In medieval Europe, as in ancient Egypt, if you were entitled to sit on a chair it meant you were important, because the chief role of furniture was to signify status.

Late-medieval sitting etiquette is illustrated in a French illumination that portrays the trial of Jean II, Duke of Alençon, a supporter of Joan of Arc. The central figure is Charles VII, who is seated on a high-backed throne. The king's twelve-year-old son is on his right, occupying a low chair that a surviving *assiette*, or seating plan, specifically describes as one foot high. Immediately in front of the king, and a few steps lower, are the chancellor and the king's constable, representing the law and the military. The pair are seated in armchairs "one just as high as the other." There are no other chairs. Arranged on the king's right and left are the leading members of the nobility and the Church, who sit on benches along the wall (being able to lean against the wall may have been considered a privilege). The members of parliament and lesser dignitaries occupy benches on descending tiers. The seating arrangement was strictly hierarchical, one's importance denoted by tier height and distance from the king. At the bottom of the social pyramid are several lawyers and legal clerks who are seated on stools, or are sprawled—unceremoniously—on the floor. The crowd of onlookers is standing.

As Fernand Braudel observed, the poor had few possessions. One looks in vain for side chairs in Pieter Brueghel the Elder's sixteenth-century paintings of peasant life—there are only stools and benches, and precious few of those. Ordinary folk mostly sit on whatever is at hand: stools, chests, up-turned buckets, or just the ground. The rediscovery of the side chair took a long time. "Fashion evolved, but in slow motion," wrote Braudel of that period. "The expense occasioned by renovation and refurnishing was enormous; more important, production possibilities remained limited." The last was critical, for despite the delicate carvings of linen fold panels and tracery, medieval joinery was relatively crude and incapable of producing the curving shapes required for true sitting comfort.

The choir stall is a representative piece of medieval sitting furniture. The overhead canopy is imposing, but the straight back and a hard flat seat offer rudimentary comfort to the sitter. The "wainscot chair" is a domestic offshoot, a boxy armchair with an elaborate carved back. Such furniture was made by the same carpenters who built houses; no wonder that the chairs exhibit an architectural solidity. Heavy and massive, they usually stood immobile against the wall.

The emergence of side chairs in the late sixteenth century was enabled by prosperity and stimulated by the growth of domesticity and the desire for light, portable furniture that would allow intimate occasions of the sort that François Boucher would later record in *Le déjeuner*. No technological breakthrough was required. The first side chairs were basically four-legged stools with the two rear legs extended to support a backrest. Simple as they were, such chairs demanded more sophisticated carpentry. As furniture-making techniques became widespread, the division between carpenters, who simply pegged wood together, and joiners, who were experts at attaching wood with complicated joints, was formalized; in London, the association of joiners received a royal charter in 1571.

By the early seventeenth century, side chairs were common

throughout Europe. These chairs were almost always padded. The invention of upholstery, which took place in the early 1600s, is an important moment in the history of the chair.* Leather or fabric was stretched over the chair's wooden frame, and stuffed with marsh grass, down, or animal hair—usually horsehair. The problem was how to keep the stuffing from shifting under use. The two most common solutions

Upholstered side chair, seventeenth century

were to quilt the upholstery into sewn compartments, or to add buttons or tufts, which were stitched completely through the upholstery and kept the stuffing in place. Padded seats could be given a pronounced domelike shape that became an important part of the chair's design. In time, upholsterers became skilled in shaping the padding and produced chairs and sofas that were almost entirely padded.

The upholstered side chair was strictly an urban chair, but it had a provincial cousin. The rustic side chair had an unpadded ladder back and a seat made out of plaited rush instead of upholstery. In England, it was sometimes called a "Dutch matted chair," suggesting that it may have been the Dutch who first wove plaited rushes directly onto the chair frame to form a seat. Wherever they originated, rush-bottomed chairs became ubiquitous, for they were extremely easy to make and did not require any special skills—or special woods. The inexpensive seats, of woven bulrushes or cattail leaves, were easily replaced when they sagged or wore

---

*The guild of upholsterers, who were originally called "upholders," was founded in 1626.

out. Uninfluenced by fashion, the model survived unchanged for centuries—and survives today.

The seventeenth-century French printmaker Abraham Bosse, whose etchings depict everyday upper-class and bourgeois interiors, populated his rooms with side chairs that are clearly status symbols as well as conveniences. Chairs appear lined up against the wall in salons, reception rooms, ballrooms, and bedchambers. They are used by ladies at dressing tables, and by musicians during evening concerts. A family says grace at the table; the youngest child sits on a folding stool, everyone else sits on a chair. A portrait painter and his subject both sit on side chairs. There were obviously no rules about how this new, versatile furniture should be used. In one Bosse etching, a romancing couple has brought a pair of chairs out onto a loggia on a fine spring day. In another, a doctor attending a woman in labor uses a chair as a stand for his medicine chest. Coats and capes are casually thrown over chairbacks. It is as if, having discovered the useful side chair, people could not get enough of it.

Apogee

We give chair parts anthropomorphic names—legs, arms, back—so it is perhaps inevitable that chairmakers should express this association in their designs. While the human leg, with its extended foot, would make a strange, Daliesque chair leg, an animal leg, with its compact paw or hoof, is more suitable. One of the oldest surviving chairs in existence, dating from the twenty-sixth century B.C., belonged to the mother of the pharaoh Cheops, who built the great pyramid at Giza. The reconstructed armchair, now in the Cairo Museum, is made of gold-plated wood decorated with papyrus flowers. The four legs are animal-shaped and rest on delicate little cat's paws, felines being revered cult figures. The legs of the chairs I saw in the Met's Egyptian gallery had similar cat's paws. The Greeks made heavy thrones with naturalistic animal legs ending in paws, hooves, or claws; sometimes the legs appear to belong to lions, sometimes to bulls. The legs of folding stools were likewise given animal shapes with visible fetlocks and hooves or paws. The Romans continued this practice, especially in table legs, whose exaggerated paws seem to belong to mythical monsters.

The ancient Chinese similarly mimicked animal shapes in their furniture. There are surviving ritual bronze vessels supported on tiger feet, and couches and tables whose legs rest on horse hooves and dragon claws. The last are usually carved grasping a pearl, which neatly solves the practical problem of how sharp claws meet the floor. While the legs of these tables are usually straight, in some cases they have a double curve that mimics the shape of a quadruped's rear leg. George Kates called this fetlock-inspired shape a "cabriole leg" because it resembled the double-curved European furniture leg. The English word *cabriole* is derived from the French *cabriolet*, a corruption of *capriole*, a particular leap in ballet. Armchairs *en cabriolet* were light enough to be picked up and moved. Such chairs generally had double-curved legs, which is the chief sense of the term in English. Since the Chinese examples date from the Ming dynasty (1368–1644) and the cabriole leg does not appear in Europe until the early eighteenth century, the resemblance is actually the other way around. The cabriole is yet another case of the Chinese getting there first.

Chinese goods arrived in Europe during the sixteenth century. The most highly prized import was porcelain, whose delicacy astonished Europeans, but chairs and tables, beautifully crafted out of extremely hard tropical woods, were also popular. These pieces were often lacquered, a technique that was unknown in the West. European cabinetmakers copied this finish, which they mistakenly termed "japanning."

The influence of China resulted in the fashion for chinoiseries, objects that were vaguely influenced by Oriental motifs. But the Chinese influence could also be profound. Cabinetmakers adopted the double-curved leg (which the British called a "hock leg" or a cabriole leg) and used it in chairs, daybeds, sofas, tables, desks, and cabinets. In some cases, the animal shape was pronounced, with the foot carved to resemble claws or talons grasping a ball, in direct imitation of the claw-and-pearl foot. A dragon's foot might even include scales. In other versions—more appealing to the modern eye—the pronounced upper knee shape and the foot-shaped swelling at the base of the leg are abstract forms. The other profound change in chair design, also copied from Chinese models, was the S-shaped splat. The splat, which replaced the traditional padded backrest, followed the natural shape of the spine and supported the lumbar region. Back splats became popular because they were comfortable, made the chair lighter, and provided the cabinetmaker an opportunity for showing off decorative carving.

These changes to the chair should not be seen in isolation. The curved splat and the graceful cabriole leg, with its sinuous convex curve above and concave curve below, appealed to the Baroque sensibility that favored what the painter William Hogarth termed the "Line of Beauty" in art, architecture, and decor. The proportions of chairs changed, the seats becoming more commodious and wider at the front. This not only provided more comfort and stability, it also created a greater visual balance. The cabriole legs, which broadened at the knee where they connected to the seat rail, no longer required stretchers, and thus stood free. Only the front legs were curved; the rear legs, rectangular and slightly splayed, were a secondary compositional element.

Vincent Scully once observed that an occupied cabriole chair disappears behind the sitter, but an unoccupied chair can seem almost alive:

> The arms curve; the splat lifts and gestures behind them. The back, with a wonderfully controlled curve, comes down and, often with a profoundly articulated hip joint, transmits its energies into the seat, which in turn transmits them to the legs. They are cabriole legs, and therefore they bend, almost crouch, and they terminate in feet of one kind or another. Eventually many of them became ball-and-claw feet, clutching and full of power. The whole chair becomes a kind of animal.

The side chair emerged first in the form of the klismos but, ignored by the Romans, it disappeared and was soon forgotten. The Middle Ages laboriously rediscovered the side chair, a crude device, not much better than the simple Cycladic chair of four thousand years earlier. The invention of upholstery improved things, but it was the influence of the ancient Chinese yokeback chair that was decisive. The cabriole chair brought

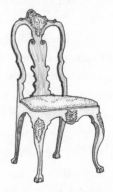

*Cabriole chair,
eighteenth century*

together several separate strands: a comfortable padded seat, delicately carved wood, a supportive splat, and expressive double-curved legs. The last, in particular, produced something not seen before in a side chair—personality.

FIVE

A Golden Age

A wing chair is a curious sort of chair. It is too vertical to be called a lounge chair, yet with its fully upholstered arms, back, and sides it is the perfect place to take a nap. We associate wing chairs with private clubs and cozy firesides, but they were originally intended for the bedroom. In fact, the first wing chairs, which appeared in England in the 1670s, were called "sleeping chayres." A pair survives in Ham House, a grand mansion on the outskirts of London: ornate chairs with open arms, padded elbow rests, carved gilded frames, crimson brocade upholstery with gold fringe, and tall upholstered wings. Both the wings and the back are adjustable by means of iron ratchets.

The Ham House chairs were specially made for a suite of rooms decorated to receive a state visit by Queen Catherine, the Portuguese wife of Charles II. Despite their richness, the chairs have an improvised look; the rectangular wings are awkwardly hinged to the back—like a pair of shutters. If these aren't the first wing chairs they are certainly very early versions. We might credit the mistress of Ham House, Elizabeth Murray, Duchess of Lauderdale, with the idea, for this exceptional woman was an inveterate domestic inventor whose kitchen included an enclosed countertop cooking stove and who installed the first private bathing room in England for her own use (baths were usually taken in tin tubs brought into the bedroom by servants).

The adjustable flaps and the reclining back of the Ham House chairs were cumbersome, but the idea of an armchair that protected the sitter from drafts proved popular. As the design was refined, the wings, arms, and back were smoothly integrated, and the entire body of the chair was padded and covered in fabric. The legs in early wing chairs were usually ornate. In the case of the Ham House chairs, the stretcher is a double scroll that includes cherubs holding bunches of grapes, and elaborately shaped legs rest on carved seahorses. Later wing chairs were simpler, and by the Georgian period, cabriole legs were common.

Details changed, but the chair retained its basic form. George Hepplewhite included a wing chair in his furniture handbook, *The Cabinet-maker and Upholsterers Guide*, which was published in 1788. He called it an easy chair, and also referred to it as a "saddle cheek," which was the traditional English term for a wing chair, because of the resemblance of the side panel to the cheekpieces of a horse's bridle.* Hepplewhite paired his chair with an adjustable "Gouty Stool," a footstool "which, by being so easily raised or lowered at either

Wing chair (after George Hepplewhite)

---

*The term "wing chair" is relatively recent. The first mention of a "wing-back chair" is in John Steinbeck's *To a God Unknown* (1933).

end, is particularly useful to the afflicted." Gout was a common eighteenth-century ailment; so were pulmonary disorders that obliged the sufferer to sleep sitting upright, for which the wing chair was well suited. The eighty-three-year-old Voltaire spent his final days in a specially made easy chair. The upholstered armchair, which is on display in the Musée Carnavalet in Paris, is on casters, and is fitted with an attached bookrest on one side and a leather-topped writing pad with a drawer on the other; both swing out of the way when not in use. On each side are pockets where the great man—busy until the end—could store papers and books.

My wing chair doesn't have a bookrest, but it would be a nice feature since I regularly use it for reading. My chair is not an antique. It was manufactured by the Hickory Chair Company of North Carolina, a firm that pioneered furniture based on eighteenth-century American models. Reproducing old furniture is not uncommon, as we have seen with the klismos. Like many Colonial wing chairs, mine has plain legs connected by stretchers. Although the padding is a combination of foam and sprung upholstery, rather than horsehair and down, the construction of my chair closely resembles its eighteenth-century predecessors: a wooden frame, padded and covered with fabric. It is the proportions and dimensions that are key. Hickory Chair once bought an expensive antique wing chair frame made by John Townsend, a famous Newport, Rhode Island, cabinetmaker, simply in order to be able to accurately reproduce its dimensions. This might seem like overkill, but it isn't. One doesn't tinker with perfection, and there is something almost magical about the chairs of that period.

The eighteenth century has been called the golden age of furniture. What makes the chairs of this period so special is a combination of highly refined technique, excellent materials, and a concern for physical comfort. It was not a matter of invention; the technical advances in upholstery and joinery had already been made—the eighteenth century merely perfected them. Prosperity assured a ready market among the growing middle class as well as the aristocracy, and widely distributed pattern books refined the taste of educated buyers and patrons. Later, the corrosive effects of the Industrial Revolution began to make themselves felt, but throughout most of the eighteenth century traditional craftsmanship prevailed, guaranteeing a level of quality in woodwork that has never been equalled, before or since. As we shall see, global trade also played a role, making first-class materials available to cabinetmakers. And what cabinetmakers they were! Just as achievements in the arts depended on the emergence of a surprising number of exceptional composers (Vivaldi, Haydn, Mozart), painters (Chardin, Reynolds, David), and writers (Pope, Voltaire, Goethe), so too in chairmaking, the creative powers of outstanding individuals made themselves felt.

Chippendale

My wing chair is based on a mid-eighteenth-century model from Virginia, but Hickory calls it the Chippendale Wing Chair, a case of marketing trumping historical accuracy. The name Chippendale is popularly associated with exceptional furniture, just as Stradivarius is associated with exceptional violins. Yet, unlike Antonio Stradivari, Thomas Chippendale did not sign his work, and except in the case of specific country houses for which he is known to have provided furniture—and whose furniture has survived—it is difficult to identify a Chippendale original.* Nevertheless, the name is used to characterize the style with which the furniture maker is associated, whether it is his work or not.

Thomas Chippendale was born in 1718 in a small town in Yorkshire. His father was a joiner and likely trained his son in the craft, although very little is known about Chippendale's youth; indeed, there is no biographical information at all concerning the first half of his life. What is known is that by the age of twenty-nine (when his marriage was recorded) he had moved to London and was the proprietor of a modest cabinetmaking shop. Somewhere along the way he learned to draw and mastered the elements of domestic design, for in addition to being a furniture maker, he appears to have been an upholsterer—as interior decorators were then called.

With the support of a wealthy Scottish backer, James Rannie, Chippendale expanded his business. He moved to fashionable St. Martin's Lane, where his neighbors were some of London's most successful cabinetmakers and upholsterers; his shop was identified by the Sign of the Chair. Rannie and Chippendale had their homes next to the shop; the workshop and lumber storage were in the rear. Chippendale prospered and employed at least twenty workers; an impressive ascent for a small-town joiner.† Like other upholsterers, he provided his clients with a full range of home furnishings: drapes, wall hangings, wallpaper, and carpets. He decorated entire country houses for wealthy landowners—

---

*Identification is further complicated by the fact that after Chippendale retired in 1777, his son—also named Thomas—continued to make furniture for another twenty-seven years.

† The largest cabinetmaker in London was George Seddon, who also started as a joiner, and who employed four hundred craftsmen in what was effectively a furniture factory.

more than two dozen such commissions are documented. Chippendale also built furniture designed by others. One of his regular clients was the Scottish architect Robert Adam, London's leading decorator. Adam was known to be extremely demanding, and that he entrusted Chippendale with commissions attests to the latter's reputation.

By Adam and Chippendale's time, Baroque had given way to rococo, forms were lighter, and surfaces were richly ornamented. The cabriole leg persisted, but in an attenuated and highly modeled form. Carving reached unprecedented heights of virtuosity. In some of Chippendale's furniture, for example, complicated details that in French furniture might have been ormolu (gilded cast bronze) were actually carved wood. This required an extremely hard material. English cabinetmakers favored imported French walnut, but in the early 1700s, after a severe winter had killed off many trees and the French government banned the export of the wood, the English began to import black walnut from Virginia and mahogany from Jamaica. This produced a momentous change in chairmaking, just as the importation of Chinese furniture to Europe had done earlier. Mahogany is harder than walnut, closer and straighter in the grain, and allows greater intricacy and crispness in carving. In addition, mahogany turns a beautiful deep red as it ages. In due course, varnished mahogany became the hallmark of English furniture.

Most of what is known about Chippendale's personal life is conjecture. Because he employed many workers, and because he executed the designs of others—notably Adam— it has been suggested that Chippendale was chiefly a businessman. His biographer Christopher Gilbert disagrees, and characterizes the cabinetmaker as "a self-made man who owed his success to ambition, opportunism, unflagging hard work and outstanding creative ability." These qualities are evident in a book that Chippendale published in 1754, just as he was launching his St. Martin's Lane enterprise. *The Gentleman and Cabinetmaker's Director* is a lavish folio volume of 160 engraved plates. The majority of the engravings are the work of Matthew Darly, an engraver and bookseller, who two years earlier had published *A New Book of Chinese, Gothic and Modern Chairs*.

The title page of Chippendale's book is a combination of self-promotion—"A Large Collection of the Most Elegant and Useful Design of Household Furniture in the Gothic, Chinese and Modern Taste"—grand promises—"Calculated to improve and refine the present TASTE, and suited to the Fancy and Circumstances of Persons in all Degrees of Life"—and sly wit: a Latin quotation from Horace, "He'll make it look like child's play, although, in fact, he tortures himself to do so."

The *Director* was available from Chippendale's shop and from booksellers in London, Edinburgh, and Dublin.* A bound copy cost two guineas, a considerable sum. The list of more than three hundred subscribers who bought advance copies (thus financing the scheme) included cabinetmakers, upholsterers, and joiners, as well as patrons. The *Director* brought Chippendale renown, but it was much more than simply a promotional tool; it was, as the name implied, a design guide. The author explained in the preface that the dual purpose of the *Director* was to serve cabinetmakers as a pattern book, and their clients as an aid in choosing furniture. For the benefit of the former, he provided precise dimensions, dimensions that were not Chippendale's personal

---

*There were two more editions. The expanded third edition was cleverly published as a succession of weekly four-plate folios at one shilling each, greatly enlarging Chippendale's readership.

invention but had been developed by furniture makers over the previous two centuries through a process of trial and error. Having described the functional model of a chair, Chippendale showed how it could be modified, using a series of drawings "which are so contrived, that if no one drawing should singly answer the Gentleman's taste, there will be found a variety of hints sufficient to construct a new one," he wrote. Thus, the thirty-eight chairs illustrated in the *Director* provided the reader with scores of alternatives for different splats, legs, and back uprights.

Chippendale's approach of mixing and matching numerous options—think what he could have done with a modern spreadsheet—underlines an important aspect of eighteenth-century chair design. Chairmakers distinguished between applied ornamental themes, which were a function of the client's taste—and his or her pocketbook—and the basic configuration of a chair, which was fixed by tradition and experience. This ensured that whatever its appearance, a chair could be counted on to provide sturdiness, stability, and comfort.

As promised, Chippendale presented three different styles: Modern, Gothic, and Chinese. The last two, probably influenced by Darly, were pure fantasy: "Gothic" had no more to do with the Middle Ages than "Chinese" had to do with the Orient. In the case of the Chinese side chairs, the geometrical motifs were not based on actual yokeback chairs but on the decorative fretwork found in folding screens and scroll paintings. Chippendale also included three "ribband-back" chairs, which had intricate splats carved in the

Ribband-back chair (after Thomas Chippendale)

shape of intertwined ribbons. He rhapsodized that these chairs were "the best I have ever seen (or perhaps have ever been made)."

The best-remembered pattern-book authors today, other than Chippendale, are George Hepplewhite and Thomas Sheraton. Their popular furniture guides went through several editions, although they lack Chippendale's authority, because no actual pieces of Hepplewhite furniture have ever been identified, and Sheraton was strictly a designer, not a cabinetmaker. So was Thomas Hope, a gifted dilettante and the author of *Household Furniture and Interior Decoration*. Nevertheless, like the *Director*, these handbooks were responsible for the spread of what was, in effect, a canon of furniture design. Thanks to these publications, provincial cabinetmakers who had no opportunity to visit a London upholsterer's showroom, let alone to see a country house interior designed by Adam or Chippendale, had at their disposal sufficient information to produce furniture of a high standard.

The Sweetness of Living

Thomas Sheraton once remarked of London cabinetmakers, "when our tradesmen are desirous to draw the best customers to their ware-rooms, they hasten over to Paris, or otherwise pretend to go there." In November 1769, Thomas Chippendale went to Paris on a shopping trip. He returned on the Calais packet, and when it docked in Dover he paid import duty on his purchases—sixty unfinished chair frames. In those days, if a customs officer suspected fraud, he had the right to confiscate the goods, pay the importer the declared value, and sell the goods at their actual price, pocketing the difference. That is what happened to Chippendale, who had declared the total value of his chair frames as eighteen pounds, even though they were worth at least three times as much. In his defense, it should be said that at the time he was in severe financial straits. His business partner, Rannie, had recently died, and to settle his estate—and his debts— Chippendale had been obliged to auction off his shop's entire stock. Moreover, several of his clients were tardy in paying their bills, leaving him hundreds of pounds out of pocket.

Chippendale planned to complete the unfinished chairs in his own workshop. It is unclear whether he bought the frames because they were cheaper or (more likely) because he wanted to get his hands on chairs in the latest neoclassical style, which was all the rage in Paris. Like couturiers in the 1950s, Parisian furniture makers in the eighteenth century led the field. French furniture-making was highly regulated. Chippendale would have purchased his chair frames from a *menuisier*, or joiner, probably from a shop in the Bonne-Nouvelle district, where most joiners lived. The French distinguished between joiners, who worked in solid wood, and cabinetmakers, or *ébénistes*, such as Jean-François Oeben, who made Madame de Pompadour's mechanical dressing table. *Ébénistes* were the aristocracy of the trade, specializing in casework (tables, desks, commodes, armoires) covered in ornamental marquetry of precious woods. Joiners provided cabinetmakers with the rough underframe for their work, and the two crafts belonged to the same guild. If a chair frame was decoratively carved, that work was done separately by a member of the carvers guild; similarly, gilt-bronze mounts required a bronzer's participation, while turned pieces came from a turner. Painting and gilding were done by separate guilds; so was upholstery. The advantage of this division of labor was that each guild maintained high standards of work-

manship and the result was exquisite furniture of exceptionally high quality.

With so many actors, who was actually responsible for
design? Sometimes joiners hired upholsterers to complete a
chair, sometimes upholsterers bought unfinished frames from
joiners and sold the finished chair on their own account.
Occasionally a customer would approach a master joiner with
a specific idea, but mostly designs originated with a third
party who acted as an intermediary between the customer
and the craftsman. This go-between might be an architect,
an artist, or an upholsterer. Upholsterers not only upholstered chairs but also supplied their customers with fabrics
for wall coverings, drapes, and carpets, and thus they assumed a key role in the decoration of houses. Another middle
man was the *marchand mercier*, or furniture dealer, who
operated outside the guild system and was purely a merchan-
diser whose fashionable showroom carried a variety of home
decorating goods. Although Diderot in his *Encyclopédie*
defined the *marchand mercier* as "seller of everything, maker
of nothing," dealers such as Lazare Duvaux, who supplied the
furnishings for Madame de Pompadour's many residences,
exercised a considerable influence on their clients' tastes.

A new idea for a chair was first presented to a customer
as a detailed, life-size drawing. After the general design
was approved, if it was an important piece, a scale model of
clay or wax was made, four to six inches high, and often incorporating alternative solutions for legs and armrests. After
these details were finalized, a carver would build a larger
wooden model, one-third actual size, showing the final chair
complete with carved ornament and even upholstery, using
fabric woven with miniature patterns. Based on this model
and accompanying drawings, a joiner would make life-size

working drawings of the various parts of the chair frame. These drawings were then transferred to wooden templates similar to a tailor's paper patterns. The templates were used to trace the outline of a piece onto the raw wood, generally beech or walnut. The roughly finished chair frame, complete with mortice-and-tenon joints, was provisionally assembled, then sent to a carver. Once he had done his work, he returned the finished parts to the joiner, who pegged, glued, and screwed them together, and smoothed down the joints.

If the chair was to be stained or polished, that work was done by the joiner; otherwise the finished frame was sent to a painter or a gilder. Gilding was more expensive than painting, not only because of the material but also because the carving had to be deeper to account for the coats of gesso that were applied as a base for the gold leaf. The final step was upholstering. Upholstery on the seat and back could be stuffed panels that were "dropped in" to the chair frame (and could be changed seasonally), or the fabric could be fixed permanently to the frame with brass tacks. The price of upholstering could equal or even exceed that of joinery and carving, depending on the quality of the fabric, such as specially woven tapestry.

A cheaper alternative to upholstery was caning, which was done either by a basketmaker or by the joiner himself. Caning is another example of the influence of Chinese techniques on European chairmaking. Caned chairs were light and airy, easy to move. They appealed to the growing desire for informality. Moreover, unlike upholstery, caning did not trap mites and fleas, an advantage in an age not known for cleanliness.

A typical joiner's workshop included the master and half a dozen journeymen, each with one or two apprentices. In the 1720s, the Parisian cabinetmakers and joiners' guild in-

Fauteuil à la reine
(Nicolas-Quinibert Foliot)

cluded almost a thousand masters; the carvers' and painters' guilds, an equal number. The cabinet-makers and joiners' guild required masters to sign their work, so the names of master chair joiners are known. Among the most celebrated were Nicolas-Quinibert Foliot, who made the armchair that Sotheby's auctioned for $653,000; Nicolas Heurtaut, the rare case of a master joiner who was also a master carver; Jean-Baptiste-Claude Sené, who regularly worked for the Garde-Meuble de la Couronne, which supplied the royal household with furnishings; Jean-Baptiste Tilliard, who, like many joiners, belonged to a family of chairmakers; and Georges Jacob, who produced the first chair *à l'anglaise*, that is, made entirely of varnished mahogany.

Eighteenth-century furniture was expensive. At a time when a journeyman joiner earned three livres a day, a good-quality armchair might cost as much as a hundred livres.* For that hefty sum, the fortunate buyer got a chair that was not only roomy, comfortable, and beautifully made, but also visually seductive. There is a story that one of the spinster daughters of Louis XV was asked why she had not entered a convent like her youngest sister. "It was an armchair that was my undoing," she replied.

In English, a chair is a chair, but in French a simple side chair is a *chaise*, while an upholstered chair with padded

---

*The cost broke down as follows: 40 percent joinery and carving, 40 percent upholstery, and 20 percent gilding.

arms is a *fauteuil*. The latter represented the acme of French furniture-making. According to Peter Thornton, curator of furniture at the Victoria and Albert Museum, "With its curvaceous and accommodating shape, and well-rounded padding on its seat, back, and arms, [the fauteuil] was one of the most satisfactory forms of seat-furniture ever devised, pleasing both to the eye and the human frame." The *fauteuil à la reine* (named in honor of the queen) was a heavy armchair that was traditionally an integral part of the design of a room, its location coordinated with the paneling, and its carving and upholstery integrated with the decor. The chair stood permanently against the wall, so the back was generally left undecorated. During the reign of Louis XV, as social customs became less formal, chair placement grew more casual. The famous painting *Reading from Molière*, by Jean-François de Troy, a contemporary of Watteau, captures such a relaxed moment. Half a dozen friends are lounging comfortably in large, low armchairs in the drawing room of a Parisian *appartement*. The heavy chairs are *fauteuils à la reine*—you can see the flat, unfinished backs—which have been moved to the center of the room and arranged in a loose circle. Three of the chairs match the silk damask on the walls, while two of them appear to have come from another room.

As informality took hold, furniture makers produced smaller and lighter fauteuils. There were several types. The *fauteuil en cabriolet* had a rounded back. The *fauteuil à coiffer* had a low back to facilitate the brushing of a lady's long hair. The bergère, or shepherdess, was a tublike armchair with closed arms, low to the ground with more generous dimensions, and often with a fitted down cushion; in other words, a very comfortable armchair. The *bergère gondole* was a tub chair whose rounded back resembled the prow of a gondola, while the wide *marquise* had continuous arms and back. The *bergère à oreilles*—a chair with ears—was the French wing chair, and was sometimes called a *bergère en confessional* because the sitter was partially hidden, as in a confessional box.

Chaises longues have already been discussed, and seating furniture included a variety of *canapés*, or sofas, which were basically stretched fauteuils. There are examples of winged settees, and *corbeille* sofas whose backs wrapped around the sides like a basket. So-called Turkish sofas were deep enough to support the legs, and were fitted with bolsters and cushions. The *canapé à confidents* was an unusual sofa with separate end seats that were either fixed or detachable. This allowed two people—the *confidents*—to have an intimate conversation, literally tête-à-tête, while decorously appearing to sit apart.

There was an astonishing variety of side chairs. Dining chairs generally had upholstered seats; backs were either decoratively slatted, caned, or upholstered. Toward the end of the century, round-back dining chairs (*en médaillon*) became popular. The *chauffeuse*, or warming chair, was a low lady's side chair, like a slipper chair, usually placed beside the

Louis XVI
voyeuse à genoux

fireplace in a bedroom. Because the study was a male preserve (Madame du Châtelet notwithstanding), desk chairs had a masculine character and were often upholstered in leather. Some had saddle-shaped seats supported by center legs, and some swiveled, the model for Jefferson's "whirligig chair." Card games were a popular pastime, and spectators would often turn a chair and straddle it, leaning on the top rail. Furniture makers produced the *voyeuse* (looking chair), whose padded rail made this position more comfortable. Card players could use a *ponteuse*, in which the padded rail held a box for one's bets (*pontes*). Ladies could hardly be expected to straddle, and they used a *voyeuse à genoux* (kneeling chair), which resembled a prie-dieu and had a seat low enough to kneel on and a taller back with a padded rail. Such chairs were also made for listening to music, and there are several examples with backs in the shape of lyres.

What was the reason for this extravagance of choice? In part, an appetite for novelty. Fashion reigned supreme, and the nature of fashion is that it changes: what is attractive and interesting in one decade becomes uninteresting and dull in the next. A chair such as the klismos had persisted for hundreds of years, but the French eighteenth century regularly produced new types of furniture such as the bergère and the *voyeuse*. Changing tastes also played a role. After thirty years, people tired of rococo and turned to a more severe neoclassicism. After only a decade, that was succeeded by the *goût arabesque*, which combined elements of both rococo and neoclassicism.

Although French chairmakers experimented with new forms of decoration, like their English counterparts they never abandoned their hard-won knowledge of joinery and ergonomics. The eighteenth century simply extended the earlier discoveries of comfortable seating by creating greater variety. There were chairs for all occasions, grand as well as casual; chairs for sitting alone as well as in groups; for sitting up, for lounging, and for reclining; different chairs for conversation, reading, playing, and napping. The variety of postures—straddling a *voyeuse*, or sinking into a bergère— reflected a less self-conscious attitude toward the human body and an awareness of the richness that life offered. Talleyrand, who served the Revolution and Napoleon, but was born during the reign of Louis XVI, understood the charms of the ancien régime. "Those who haven't lived in the eighteenth century before the Revolution do not know the sweetness of living," he once observed. *La douceur de vivre.*

SIX

Sack-backs and Rockers

In the late seventeenth century, people living in the American colonies who wanted fine furniture had to import it from England. But by the early 1700s, they had their own cabinetmakers. The leading center of furniture-making was Boston, followed—and in the latter half of the eighteenth century surpassed—by Philadelphia. Smaller cities such as Newport, Rhode Island, also developed local expertise. Furniture was exported to other coastal colonies: Maryland, Virginia, the Carolinas, and Georgia. As early as 1730, decades before the appearance of Chippendale's pattern book, Boston cabinetmakers were producing side chairs with cabriole legs (called bandy legs) and ball-and-claw feet (called crowfeet) that rivaled English models for quality. New World cabinetry was facilitated by the availability of hardwoods—black walnut from Pennsylvania and Virginia, as well as Jamaican mahogany, which was used long before it became popular in England. After mid-century, English pattern books enabled American cabinetmakers to keep up with the latest fashions. Chippendale's *Director* was popular, as was Robert Manwaring's *The Cabinet and Chair Maker's Real Friend and Companion*, which was published in Boston only two years after it appeared in London.

A ready supply of hardwoods is hardly sufficient to explain the accomplishments of colonial furniture makers. A new demand for high-quality furniture was part of a broad cultural change. The historian Richard L. Bushman has described the process of refinement that began in 1700 as the consequence not simply of greater prosperity and fashion consciousness, but of a genuine and widespread desire for gentility. This desire manifested itself in many different ways, not least the impulse to beautify one's surroundings, especially one's home. "Men of substance everywhere occupied themselves with the details of architecture, furniture design, and landscaping," writes Bushman.

The leading "man of substance"—in many ways a national model—was George Washington. In 1757, he began to enlarge his house at Mount Vernon and to beautify its grounds, and over the next three decades he made it into a twenty-room mansion that was one of the larger houses in Virginia. He furnished the rooms with a variety of chairs from many sources. One of his earliest acquisitions was six used black walnut Chippendale-style side chairs, which he bought from a fellow officer while he was serving in the Virginia militia. Later, he ordered a dozen mahogany side chairs from his English agent in London; the wing chair in his and Martha's bedroom came from an English auction house. In 1790, Washington bought several fauteuils and a bergère with a footstool from the Comte de Moustier, the departing French ambassador.

The impressive main room at Mount Vernon rises the full two-story height of the house. Decorated in the Adamesque style, this salon was used for socializing, receptions, and dancing, and also functioned as a banqueting room—when a temporary table was set up on trestles. The room contained two dozen Sheraton-style mahogany side chairs as well as two grand sideboards, all made by John Aitken, a Scottish-born Philadelphia cabinetmaker. The chairs in the adjacent parlor were Chippendale-style mahogany cabriole side chairs, similar to the ones that Thomas Burling, a New York cabinetmaker, had supplied for Washington's official residence when the federal capital was in New York City. Burling made the side chairs in the family dining room.

Washington's study contained a mahogany dressing table that he had bought from de Moustier, and a handsome tambour secretary made by Aitken. At the secretary stood an upholstered barrel-back swivel chair. Washington recorded that he paid Burling seven pounds for the "Uncom^n Ch^r." Such swivel chairs were indeed uncommon in America though not, as we have seen, in France—perhaps Washington came across one in de Moustier's study. A month later, not to be outdone, Jefferson ordered his own swivel chair, the infamous "whirlgig chair," with a taller back and bright red leather upholstery (Washington's chair was black). Jefferson also added two "candle arms," so that when he swiveled, light would follow. Different men, different chairs.

The Stick Chair

Washington had another unusual chair in his study. The chair at his writing desk was fitted with an overhead pasteboard fan that swung back and forth like an Indian punkah, the power being supplied by the sitter using a foot treadle. The inventor of the "Fan Chair" was John Cram, a Philadelphia musical instrument maker, who had built the first one in 1786 for the artist Charles Willson Peale and later made one for Benjamin Franklin. Cram built the support frame and the treadle mechanism; the chair itself was an ordinary Windsor, the most common chair of that time.

The Windsor chair is an English invention. The key to its ingenious design is the seat, a thick slab of solid hardwood, carved with two shallow, saddle-shaped depressions to provide sitting comfort. The back hoop is a single piece of wood, steam-heated and bent into shape. The hoop is simply countersunk into the seat, as are the turned spindles and splayed legs—no complicated joinery or hardware is required. Although there are rare examples of mahogany chairs, English Windsors were generally made of a combination of commonplace woods: hard elm for the seat, dense beech for the turnings, and malleable ash or yew for the hoop. Windsor chairs were inexpensive—an unpainted chair sold for a few shillings, compared with more than a pound for a Chippendale-style mahogany side chair. They were used in taverns and public houses, and in the homes of ordinary country people; in wealthier households they served as outdoor furniture.

The Windsor chair originated in the late seventeenth century in Buckinghamshire, whose extensive beechwood forests provided a ready supply of material for the turnings. There is a charming story that George II came across the chair while sheltering from the rain in a cottage and found it so comfortable that he ordered several for Windsor Castle, which gave the chair its name. Unfortunately, it is only a story, because there are textual references to "Windsor chairs" years before George II assumed the throne. The name more likely derived either from Windsor Great Forest, whence much of the wood originated, or from the market town of Windsor, which was a clearinghouse for the chairs on their way to London.

English hoop-back
Windsor chair

Windsor chairs were produced by a cottage industry. Bolgers, who lived in the forest, used pedal-operated pole-lathes to turn the spindles, legs, and stretchers. Bottomers carved the seats, benchmen produced the splats and sawn parts, while polishers smoothed the rough pieces with spokeshaves and sandpaper. Framers assembled the parts, and stainers finished the chair, typically black or green. None of these techniques were particularly novel; they were adapted from the wheelwright's craft, which traditionally steam-bent wood for wheel rims, used lathe-turned spindles for spokes, and drilled holes for socket joints.

There were two basic types of Windsor chairs: the hoop-back, in which a steam-bent hoop supported the spindles, and the comb-back, in which the spindles themselves supported a carved crest rail. There were many permutations: with arms, with splats, with V-shaped back braces, with a low or a high back, and with straight, turned, or cabriole legs. What all these chairs had in common was that they were light, strong, and comfortable.

The Windsor chair arrived in America very early. Patrick Gordon, who was deputy governor of the Province of Pennsylvania and the Lower Counties on the Delaware, brought five comb-back Windsor chairs with him when he arrived in Philadelphia in 1726. This plain chair must have appealed to the frugal Quakers, for there were soon scores of Windsor chairmakers in the city. The most popular model was the hoop-back, known locally as a sack-back. These so-called Philadelphia chairs were exported to other colonies up and down the eastern seaboard and as far south as the West Indies. It is easy to understand the Windsor chair's appeal: it did not use fancy woods; it did not require wood-carving or upholstering skills; unlike a rush chair the seat never had to be replaced; and an old chair needed only a coat of paint to freshen it up. By mid-century, the Windsor chair was the most popular chair in the colonies. Windsor chairs furnished Philadelphia's Carpenters' Hall, where the First Continental Congress met, and the State House, where the Founding Fathers gathered to sign the Declaration of Independence and the Constitution.*

American Windsor chairs were not produced by a rural cottage industry but in cities, and although some of the production approached the organization of an assembly line, the best were made by individual craftsmen, such as Francis Trumble, Joseph Henzey, and Thomas Gilpin, all of Philadelphia. Some of these men started as cabinetmakers, others specialized in Windsor chairs, and all were skilled craftsmen (often signing their chairs). American makers of Windsor chairs did not—in fact, could not—copy English models, for this humble chair was not included in pattern books. Consequently, they were free to exercise their own ingenuity, and in the process produced chairs that reached a higher level of refinement than their English counterparts. Splats and cabriole legs were done away with, and spindles were made progressively thinner. Comb-backs were given interesting scrolls, and the ends of arms were often carved with

---

*When John Trumbull, who trained in London, painted *The Declaration of Independence*, which appears on the back of the two-dollar bill, he replaced the common sack-backs with upholstered armchairs. Junius Brutus Stearns and Howard Chandler Christy followed this convention in their painted depictions of the signing of the U.S. Constitution. In fact, the only "fancy" chair in the Assembly Room of Independence Hall was the speaker's Chippendale-style armchair.

knuckles resembling animal paws. Some makers combined the sack-back and the comb-back to make an especially tall chair with a headrest. The lightest, most delicate model was the fan-back armchair, whose tall sloping back was reinforced by two diagonal braces. The prices of these chairs varied: a plain sack-back might cost only a few shillings, whereas a respected maker could demand as much as fifteen shillings.

After mid-century, Windsor chair manufacturing spread to New York and New England. Ebenezer Stone, a Boston maker of "Warranted Green Windsor Chairs," advertised that his chairs were "painted equally as well as those made in Philadelphia." Chairmakers in New York City developed a particularly elegant design in which the hoop-back and the arms were made out of one continuous steam-bent piece of hickory or ash. Because elm was rare, American makers generally used poplar or pine for the seat, and maple for the spindles. As in England, Windsor chairs were either stained or painted—green was popular, so were red and black.

There is nothing rustic about American Windsor chairs, which were as likely to furnish a grand house as a roadside tavern. Jefferson owned more than twenty of them. What he called "stick chairs" stood in the entrance hall of Monticello and were moved around the house as required. He also owned an unusual revolving Windsor chair, in which he is said to have written the Declaration of Independence. Revolving Windsor chairs did not become common until the 1840s, so it is likely that Jefferson himself

Continuous-arm Windsor chair with bamboo legs

designed this chair. Washington, too, owned many Windsor chairs. He bought two dozen oval-back Windsor side chairs with fashionable "bamboo" legs from a Philadelphia maker, and placed them on the porch at Mount Vernon; he had the Windsor fan chair in his study, a Windsor armchair in his bedroom, and a Windsor high chair for his grandchildren. The most unusual of Washington's Windsors was his "riding chair," a cannibalized Windsor chair seat bolted to the frame of a two-wheeled horse-drawn buggy.

The American Windsor chair had many specialized offspring. Windsor settees ranged in length from four to twelve feet. Windsor writing-arm chairs had one arm broadened into an oval writing surface. In some versions, the writing arm had a drawer for paper, pens, and ink; the sewing Windsor had a drawer under the seat. The smoker's bow was a stocky chair with wide arms on which a pipe smoker could rest his elbow. The captain's chair was another low-back Windsor chair, as was the firehouse Windsor. Stools, with three or four legs, were available in a variety of heights. Perhaps the humblest Windsor chair was the stick-back kitchen chair, similar to my flea-market side chairs. Here the design was reduced to its plainest and most utilitarian essentials: a solid shaped seat, a simple comb-back, turned legs and spindles.

When I arrived at the University of Pennsylvania two decades ago, my office was unfurnished, and I was asked what kind of chairs I would like. I chose Windsor chairs—a sack-back armchair for myself, and a bow-back side chair for visitors. The seat was pine, the turned pieces maple, and the bow-back ash. The Warren Chair Works of Warren, Rhode Island, which made my chairs, uses programmed lathes and electrical-powered cutting and drilling machines, instead of pole lathes, pit saws, and carpenter's braces, but the design of my armchair is virtually identical to the sack-back that

Benjamin Franklin occupies in Robert Edge Pine's eighteenth-century painting *Congress Voting Independence*.

Windsor chairs have been mass-produced since the nineteenth century, and although purists might consider the handmade versions superior, the design of the Windsor chair proved remarkably durable and unlike many handcrafted artifacts it survived industrialization intact. The explanation is simple. "In anything at all, perfection is finally attained not when there is no longer anything to add, but when there is no longer anything to take away, when a body has been stripped down to its nakedness," observed Antoine de Saint-Exupéry. He was describing an airplane, but his observation applies equally to a Windsor chair. Everything extraneous has been removed; no matter how it is fabricated—in a workshop or in a factory—the result is the same. A Windsor chair is not made of fine woods, and it doesn't need to be decorated; its appeal is entirely a function of its proportions and its air of lightness and grace.

Wooden Narcotics

If the Windsor chair could be said to be England's national chair, the quintessential American chair is the rocking chair. Like the Windsor chair, the rocking chair originated as a vernacular product, that is, it was the work of anonymous chairmakers. Nothing could be simpler than adding two curved rockers to an ordinary chair; after all, cradles have had rockers since the Middle Ages. Then why did it take several centuries before someone did it to a chair? Part of the explanation may be the lack of a suitably light and inexpensive chair; medieval armchairs were too heavy, and backstools did not lend themselves to rocking. More important, the symbolic function of chairs precluded adding something as carefree as a rocking motion. It's hard to imagine a cabriole chair or a fauteuil on rockers. For hundreds of years chairs were associated with stability and repose—a chair that rocked back and forth would have seemed undignified.

To a colonial settler living in the wilderness of North America and largely cut off from the conventions of the Old World, a chair that rocked might have appeared slightly less preposterous. Or at least worth trying. Benjamin Franklin owned a rocking chair but he was not its inventor. The earliest record of a rocking chair is a 1742 invoice written by Solomon Fussell, a Philadelphia cabinetmaker who charged six shillings for "one Nurse Chair with rockers." Nurse chairs, which were common at that time, were low armless side chairs used by wet nurses and nursing mothers. We don't know what Fussell's rocking nurse chair looked like, but judging from the low price it must have been rather plain, probably with a ladder back and a rush bottom.

Infants are lulled to sleep by a gently rocking motion—whether in a mother's arms or in a cradle—so a rocking nurse chair makes sense. Fussell, with a Quaker's taste for simplicity, would certainly have appreciated the idea, but he cannot be credited with the invention. Shortly after he made the nurse chair, a "rocking chair" was listed in the estate of a deceased Chester County, Pennsylvania, resident, which suggests an earlier origin, probably sometime in the early 1700s.

The first rocking chairs were used by nursing mothers, and were also considered suitable for the elderly

Ladder-back, rush-bottom rocking chair

and the infirm. However, as people realized that such chairs were an inexpensive alternative to upholstered easy chairs, their popularity grew, and by 1750, rush-bottom rocking chairs had spread from Pennsylvania to New England. Before the turn of the century, rockers were being attached to Windsor chairs. A Windsor rocker cost about twice as much as a rush-bottom rocker, but with its carved seat, ample width, and sloping back it was considerably more comfortable.

By the 1820s, rocking chairs had become a national fad; every American home had at least one. They were as likely to be found in the parlor as in the bedroom or kitchen. Or on the porch—porches facing the street were a distinctive feature of American houses, and rocking chairs were tailor-made for people-watching. One of the most popular rocking chairs was the Boston rocker, a comb-back Windsor chair with a tall back surmounted by a broad top rail that provided comfortable support for the head—and a convenient location for decoration, usually stenciled floral motifs. The spindles of the back were sometimes gently curved in an S shape, and the arms were generally heavy and ended in scrolls. Some Boston rockers had elaborate seats that curved down at the front and up at the rear.

Boston rocker

Foreigners were struck—and amused—by the American habit of rocking back and forth. The writer Frances Trollope described women living in a Philadelphia boarding-house: "As to what they do . . . it is not very easy to say; but I believe they clear-starch a little, and iron a little, and sit in a rocking-chair and sew a great deal." Another nineteenth-century British visitor described the rocking chair as "of exclusive American contrivance and use," and commented on the "comfort and luxurious ease of these wooden narcotics." Philip Schaff, a Swiss theologian who spent most of his life in the United States, went further and considered the rocking chair to be a reflection of national character. "Even when seated, [Americans] push themselves to and fro in their rocking chairs," he wrote in 1854; "they live in a state of perpetual excitement in their business, their politics, and their religion . . ."

Alexis de Tocqueville, who visited America in the 1830s, had nothing to say about rockers but he did record an insight that bears on chairs. Always on the lookout for differences between America and France, he pointed out that in aristocratic France an accomplished artisan could sell his skills to the elite at a high price, whereas in a democracy the mass market required vastly reduced prices. "But there are only two ways of lowering the price of commodities," he wrote. "The first is to discover some better, shorter, and more ingenious method of producing them; the second is to manufacture a larger quantity of goods, nearly similar, but of less value." Tocqueville was certainly correct about what drove the difference between a *fauteuil à la reine* and a sack-back Windsor chair, but reducing prices is not the only way to attract buyers in a mass market. Another is novelty. No sooner did the rocking chair become popular than chairmakers began offering unusual options: a rocking chair for invalids with a superstructure frame over which a protective blanket could be draped, turning it into an improvised wing chair; baby rockers for children and medium-size rockers for youths; settee rockers for two; a settee rocker with a fence insert that transformed the space next to the mother into a cradle. Samuel May of Sterling, Massachusetts, patented a rocker in which the seat and one arm slid sideways to make the chair wider, and the removable headpiece was inserted into the front of the seat, converting the rocking chair into a baby's cradle.

The line between chairmaker and chair inventor was often blurred. Samuel Gragg was an enterprising joiner who learned how to steam-bend wood while making continuous-arm Windsor chairs as an apprentice in New York City. After he opened his own furniture shop in Boston in 1801, he made Windsor chairs and rocking chairs with delicate S-shaped back splats (which would influence the design of Boston rockers). He also experimented with steam-bending, and in 1808 patented a chair made entirely out of extremely thin pieces of bent wood. It is a remarkable design: the front legs curve up to form the edge of the seat, and curve again to form the back support; the back splats and the seat are made of continuous pieces. He called it the Elastic Chair. Although a few dozen examples survive in museums today, the chair was not a commercial success. "The Elastic Chair was simply too labor and skill intensive to be financially successful," Michael Podmaniczky, a Delaware chairmaker and restorer, who is an authority on Gragg, wrote to me in an

e-mail. Podmaniczky has built several Elastic Chairs, both for exhibitions and for his own use, and I asked him what the delicate-looking chairs were like to sit in. "They are as comfortable as a solid wood chair can be. As for their strength, they are superior to most." Is the chair really elastic? "No. It's actually quite stiff," he answered. "Gragg was thinking of the pliable wood after steaming when he named it." As we shall see

Elastic Chair
(Samuel Gragg)

in the following chapter, it would be left to another inventor to perfect a chair made out of bentwood.

The rocking chair took many forms: Windsor chair, Boston rocker, rush-bottomed chair, rattan and wicker chair. Early in the nineteenth century, fully upholstered parlor rockers appeared, with tufted backs, padded armrests, and mahogany frames. It was in such a chair that President Lincoln was assassinated in Ford's Theatre.

The rocking chair never went out of fashion, but the homely rocker acquired an unexpected glamor in the 1960s, thanks to President Kennedy. As a senator, Kennedy had chronic back pain, and his doctor prescribed sitting in a rocking chair. The chair alleviated Kennedy's lower-back tension by contracting and relaxing the muscles—a wooden narcotic, indeed. The particular model the doctor recommended to the president was—and is—manufactured by a small company in North Carolina. The traditional high-back design, which dates from the late 1920s, uses an oak frame to support a woven cane seat and has a distinctive caned backrest. President Kennedy had fourteen of these chairs, and used them in the Oval Office, the White House bedroom, Camp David, his summer house at Hyannis Port, and even on Air Force One.

The rocking chair, like touch football, became a popular symbol of the Kennedy presidency, not least because it was perceived—correctly—to be quintessentially American. The rocker is a chair that is equally at home on the front porch of a cabin in the Ozarks and on the balcony of the White House.* Like the klismos, which it doesn't resemble in the least, it is a democratic chair.

---

*Kennedy was hardly the first president to bring a rocking chair into the White House. Lincoln favored rockers; McKinley had one; so did Theodore Roosevelt. Coolidge kept one on the porch, and Truman had several on the first-floor balcony that he added to the rear portico.

SEVEN

The Henry Ford of Chairs

One of the first chairs you need, when furnishing a new home, is a dining chair. You can make do with cushions on the floor instead of an easy chair, as I did in my first apartment, and you can read a book or watch television lying in bed, but if you are going to eat at a table you need something to sit on. Early in our marriage and shortly after we had finished building our house, my wife and I decided to replace our collection of beat-up side chairs, accumulated separately over the years, with proper dining chairs. I knew what I wanted. I had a bentwood-and-cane chair in my university office. I had used it for several years so I knew it was comfortable, and I liked the way it looked.

We visited a furniture distributor in the east end of Montreal who carried bentwood chairs. The one I wanted turned out to be pricier than we expected—or could afford—so we looked at other models that were on display in the showroom. We were attracted to a bentwood chair with a curved hoop for the back, thin slats, a circular bentwood leg brace, all stained black. It was not quite as elegant as our first choice, and the padded seat was not as pretty as woven

cane, but I knew from experience that cane would eventually sag and need to be replaced. This armless side chair was
affordable, and equally important, with a taller back it offered better support and was actually more comfortable.
The dealer offered a reduced price if we took eight of them,
so we did. More than thirty years later they continue to
serve.

Our dining chairs are stamped MADE IN CZECHOSLOVA-
KIA on the underside of the frame. Czechoslovakia has been
associated with bentwood furniture since the mid-nineteenth
century, when bentwood chair factories appeared in the
beechwood forests of Moravia (today a part of the Czech
Republic but then a province of the Austro-Hungarian Empire). The man responsible for these factories looms large in
the history of the chair. He transformed furniture-making,
from a craft practiced by individual cabinetmakers in workshops, to an industry operating on a world scale.

Michael Thonet was born in 1796 in Boppard, a small
town in the Palatinate, a border region of France but soon
to become a part of Prussia. He came from a modest
background—his father was a tanner—and as a boy he was
apprenticed to a cabinetmaker.* Eventually, he opened his
own shop in Boppard, making furniture by hand in the time-
tested way. Thonet was ambitious and inventive, and he began experimenting with laminated veneers, cutting wood
into thin strips, boiling bundles of strips in glue, and bending them in molds. His earliest applications were curved
headboards, baseboards for sofas, and back rails for chairs;
his first large commission was cartwheels for the Prussian
military. By 1836 he was making entire chairs out of bent

---

*The family was of Huguenot descent, but the name is pronounced in German
"Tawn-net."

veneer. Bentwood chairs required less material and labor and were cheaper to produce than hand-carved chairs, and because laminated wood was stronger they could be extremely light and graceful.

Thonet was not the first to explore bending laminated wood. Samuel Gragg had produced the Elastic Chair almost thirty years earlier, and Jean-Joseph Chapuis of Brussels, a Paris-trained master joiner, developed a technique for steambending laminated wood at about the same time. Chapuis served an exclusive clientele—he furnished the royal castle of Laeken in Brussels—and his delicate neoclassical chairs of laminated mahogany and beech are very beautiful; the curved legs recall those of a curule chair. It is unlikely that Thonet, a provincial cabinetmaker, would have known of Chapuis's work, any more than he would have heard of Gragg in far-off Boston. The Boppard craftsman seems to have arrived at the technique on his own.

In 1841, a display of Thonet's unusual furniture at a craft fair in Koblenz caught the eye of Prince Klemens von Metternich, chancellor of the Austro-Hungarian Empire. Impressed by Thonet's handiwork, the noted statesman invited the cabinetmaker to his nearby country estate—Thonet showed up with several bentwood samples: a chair, a cartwheel, and a walking stick. Metternich convinced his guest to visit Vienna, where, with the chancellor's support, Thonet received a furniture order from Emperor Franz Josef. More important, Thonet was granted an Austrian patent for his woodbending process.

Back in Boppard, things were not going well. Thonet had borrowed heavily to finance patent applications in Britain, France, and Belgium, and his impatient creditors forced him into bankruptcy. Finally, the penniless cabinetmaker and his large family—he had five sons and six daughters—immigrated to Vienna. It took Thonet several years to get back on his feet. While working for a Viennese furniture maker, he produced laminated wood flooring and exquisitely delicate laminated wood chairs for wealthy clients. But his real aim was to develop a light, inexpensive chair for a very different market: the growing number of restaurants and coffeehouses in the city.

When he was finally in a position to reopen his own workshop, his first customer was the fashionable Café Daum in Vienna, which he supplied with side chairs and coat stands. This was followed by an order for five hundred chairs from a Budapest hotel. Thonet's café chairs were exceedingly simple in design: round caned seats, independent front legs, and a single curved piece forming the rear legs and the backrest. The pieces were made of veneered mahogany—four veneers for the back and legs and five for the seat ring. By now Thonet had refined his technique, and the wood strips were first boiled in water, bent and allowed to dry, then glued together. A commercial chair takes a lot of punishment, and perhaps the greatest testament to Thonet's process is that the Café Daum chairs are said to have remained in continuous use for thirty years.

Shortly after the Café Daum, Thonet received a commission from the princely Schwarzenberg family to provide fancy side chairs for their palace in Vienna. The breathtakingly slender chairs are very beautiful. Similar chairs, together with a settee and side tables, were displayed by Thonet at the Great Exhibition of 1851 in London's Crystal Palace. The exhibition jury, not quite sure what to make of this novel furniture, which was obviously not made by hand in the traditional manner, awarded the "curious chairs" second prize. Prizes in trade fairs in Munich and Paris followed.

The furniture market had changed in the hundred years

since Chippendale, and goods now moved regularly between countries. Orders for bentwood chairs started coming to Thonet from the far-flung reaches of the Austro-Hungarian Empire, from continental Europe, and from even farther afield. It was the South American trade that led to his crucial technical breakthrough. Thonet was getting complaints that during shipment chairs were delaminating because the glue was affected by maritime humidity. The obvious solution was to replace the laminations with solid wood. Although all his previous attempts at bending solid pieces of wood into tight curves had ended in failure, Thonet persevered. He invented a technique that involved clamping a metal strip to the wood, to relieve the pressure as the piece was bent. In 1856, he was granted a patent for this crucial invention. That gave the company thirteen years of exclusive rights over the bending process.

Michael Thonet's bentwood chairs, which were considerably cheaper than conventional furniture, were a commercial success. Within five years he had two Viennese workshops employing more than a hundred cabinetmakers and craftsmen. However, they couldn't keep up with demand, so Thonet set out to build a full-fledged chair factory. The first challenge was the raw material. Although in the past he had used a variety of tropical woods, including mahogany and Brazilian rosewood, he wanted a local source. Copper beech, suitable for bending, grew abundantly in the forests of neighboring southern Moravia, and he chose the small market town of Koritschan (today Koryčany) as the site for the factory. He organized the production process into a series of discrete steps. First, beechwood logs were cut into strips that were then turned on a lathe. The round pieces were steamed until pliable, and bent to shape in cast-iron molds. Once dried, which took at least twenty-four

hours, the pieces were taken out
of the molds, sanded, and stained.
These operations did not require
skilled labor—the factory employed
no cabinetmakers or carpenters.
Local men did the heavy work of
bending, women the lighter tasks
of sanding, staining, and caning.
When the Koritschan factory was up
and running, three hundred workers
could turn out as many as fifty
thousand chairs a year. Even so, soon

*No. 14 café chair
(Michael Thonet)*

additional factories were needed and three were built in
Moravia as well as a fifth in Hungary.

The cover of the first Thonet catalog, published in 1859,
carried the proud motto *Beigen oder Brechen*, To Bend or to
Break. The broadsheet illustrated twenty-six products: chairs,
settees, and tables. The chairs were designed with interchangeable parts, so that different models could be created
by recombining assorted backs and arms. Number 14, a café
chair, was the least expensive item; it sold for three Austrian
florins, about the price of a bottle of good wine. Known as
the *Konsumstuhl*, or Consumer's Chair, No. 14 was the
workhorse of the Thonet line. The design had been reduced
to absolute basics. There were only six pieces: a caned seat,
two front legs, a single curved piece that formed the rear legs
and the back, a circular leg brace, and a curved back insert.
That makes the design sound utilitarian, but it wasn't; the
slender legs tapered and flared gracefully and the circular
leg brace echoed the round seat. The absence of decoration
gave it a timeless quality that makes No. 14, in its own way,
as enduring as the klismos or the cabriole chair.

Thonet chairs left the factory disassembled. They were

shipped flat and put together after delivery. Assembly was simple; the six pieces of a No. 14 chair, for example, required only ten screws and two washers (the hardware was manufactured by Thonet, too). Thirty-six disassembled chairs could be packed into a compact crate only one meter a side. Flat-packing, as much as ingenious design and rationalized production, accounted for the remarkable success of Thonet's chairs.

Michael Thonet died in 1871; he was seventy-five. Photographs of him in later life show a handsome man with longish hair and a full white beard; he resembles Karl Marx, another Rhineland Palatinate native. The resemblance ends there, for Thonet was an early example of the capitalist-entrepreneur. Fifty years before Henry Ford introduced the Model T automobile assembly line in Highland Park, Thonet had already put in place the basic elements of mass production: division of labor, interchangeable parts, mechanization. As Ford would later do, he integrated his business vertically, buying forest land, laying railroad track, operating his own sawmills, and building his own machine saws, steam retorts, and iron molds. He even manufactured the bricks that were used to build the worker housing, schools, and libraries in his company towns. He must have been something of a benevolent despot, for he required his workers to use "Thonet currency" in the company stores. The firm's offices were housed in an ornate seven-story block on fashionable Stephansplatz in Vienna. From there, the family directed its international operations. There were showrooms in all the major European cities: London, Paris, Berlin, Rotterdam, Hamburg, Vienna, Budapest, Prague, and Brno.

Michael Thonet is a landmark figure. Not only did he invent a new technique for making chairs—and design beautiful chairs to suit that technique—he also put in place an industrialized method of mass production and global mass marketing. What is unexpected is that unlike the firearm or the automobile, which were also early products of industrialization, the chair was a traditional artifact whose basic form dated back thousands of years. It was an unlikely candidate for one of the first mass-produced objects of the Industrial Age—a consumer's chair, indeed.

The Brothers Thonet

When Thonet formally registered his company, he named it Gebrüder Thonet (Thonet Brothers), and made his five sons, all of whom had joined him in the business, co-owners. After his death, the company continued to thrive under their direction. Number 18 replaced No. 14 as the ubiquitous café chair—it appears in Toulouse-Lautrec's painting *At the Moulin Rouge*. This chair has a larger back insert that provides additional support and stability for a fractionally higher price; the design is also more comfortable because the backpiece does not touch the spine. By 1904, No. 14 shared space in the Thonet catalogue (which appeared in five languages) with no fewer than 1,270 items, domestic as well as commercial. The astonishing assortment included garden furniture, tip-up theater seats—the first of their kind—and such specialized items as barstools, piano stools, and barber's chairs. There was a concert-hall chair with a hat rack under the seat, and a dressing-room chair with a boot jack. The company also manufactured coat stands, easels, magazine racks, and an assortment of walking-stick seats.

Mass production is based on mass consumption, and reaching a wide market meant offering a large variety of products. This was very different from the output of eighteenth-century joiners and cabinetmakers, who were supplying a relatively narrow social class, albeit one interested in novelty. Mass marketing was obliged to cater to diverse tastes. The café chairs came with a variety of decorative back inserts and armrests, imitation intarsia seats, and assorted curlicue additions. The most famous Thonet chairs today are in the curvaceous Art Nouveau style, but the company also offered traditional German peasant furniture, versions of Windsor chairs, a Renaissance-style scissors chair, Gothic chairs, even a line of exotic furniture with bentwood imitating bamboo. One of the most curious models used spiral-cut bentwood in imitation of wrought iron. Thonet also developed special designs for particular export markets. For France, there was a smoker's chair that resembled a *ponteuse*, with a padded rest across the top rail and a box for storing smoking supplies; for the United States, swiveling counter seats for bars, soda fountains, and luncheonettes, and chairs with reinforced back legs to account for the peculiarly American habit of tilting back a chair on its rear legs.

At the 1851 Crystal Palace exhibition, British manufacturers had displayed innovative metal rocking chairs quite unlike American rockers. The British designs visually integrated the rockers with the curved arms and backs, so they looked all of a piece. Michael Thonet had been impressed by this fluid design, and soon the company was producing a variety of similar rockers in bentwood. The chairs were elegant and light, especially when the upholstery was replaced by woven cane. The ultimate Thonet rocker was the *Schaukensofa*, or rocking sofa. It is a rocking chaise longue with a caned seat and an adjustable reclining back. Often described as the most elegant of all the nineteenth-century bentwood chairs, it is a paragon of wood-bending techniques: two sinuous pieces of wood, each more than seventeen feet long

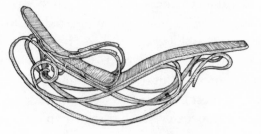

Schaukensofa
(*August Thonet*)

(butt-jointed in the middle), curve and recurve upon themselves to form the rockers and sides.

Rocking chairs had not been popular in Europe until the
Thonet rockers came along.* Their sinuous form appealed
particularly to artists, and Thonet rockers feature in paintings by Renoir, Vuillard, and Tissot. The connection between
painters and Thonet rockers was so strong that it persisted
well into the 1950s; Picasso and Miró kept Thonet rockers in
their studios and the chairs appear in several of their canvases.

August Thonet, the third son, succeeded his father as the
creative force behind Gebrüder Thonet. He is credited with
the design of the *Schaukensofa*. Another of his virtuoso designs was a demonstration chair made for the Paris Exposition
Universelle of 1867: two extremely long pieces of bentwood
intertwine to form one apparently continuous line. He also
designed an experimental side chair made out of a single
precut plank of wood that was progressively bent to form
the finished chair. More prosaically, he invented a veneered
wooden seat for the café chair that was longer-lasting and
less expensive than woven cane, and braced the frame, making the entire chair stronger.

---

*The exception was Sweden and Denmark, where rocking chairs were intro-
duced by emigrants returning from America.

On the eve of World War I, Gebrüder Thonet was producing 1.8 million items annually, three-quarters of them
chairs. The brothers were as driven as their father, and production facilities expanded to keep pace with increased
international demand. There were now seven factories, not
only in Moravia and Hungary but also in Germany, Galicia,
and Russian-occupied Poland. By now, the bentwood patents had expired, and the company faced stiff competition,
notably from Mundus and Jacob & Josef Kohn, both of
Vienna. In 1914, Mundus merged with Kohn, and eight
years later they were joined by Thonet, forming the largest
furniture conglomerate in the world. Thonet—the new company continued to use the old name—did not rest on its bentwood laurels, however, and as we shall see in the following
chapter, in the interwar years Thonet would emerge, yet
again, as a leading manufacturer of innovative furniture.

Sitzmaschine

Gebrüder Thonet had always designed its own chairs. Although individual designers were not named, it is generally
assumed that in the early days Michael Thonet was the primary designer, and that after his death that responsibility
passed to August. This began to change in 1899, when the
architect Adolf Loos approached the company with a custom
order for a café chair, to furnish the fashionable Café Museum in central Vienna. Loos's design was a variation on the
standard Thonet chair, but with significant modifications:
the rear legs extended to form the back insert while the top
rail was a separate piece that was attached to the seat; the legs
were braced by four separate pieces. The back had a wave
shape instead of a simple arch. In addition, Loos specified an

oval cross-section instead of the usual round dowel. Whether the form of this complicated chair really followed function, as Loos claimed, is debatable. Thonet did not add Loos's design to its catalogue, probably because it was unsuited to mass production, but there was no denying that the Café Museum chair was striking. Loos had made the bentwood café chair, now forty years old, seem fresh and up-to-date.

A few years later, when Otto Wagner, the dean of Austrian avant-garde architects, was building the Postsparkasse, the headquarters of the Post Office Savings Bank in Vienna, a seminal building of the Secession movement, he likewise furnished it with Gebrüder Thonet bentwood chairs of his own design. Wagner's side chairs and armchairs had very simple geometrical shapes, and they were a radical departure from tradition: instead of a round dowel he specified a square cross-section, and he gave it an ebonized finish (previously bentwood chairs had been stained). One of Wagner's most memorable designs was a stool for public use in the main banking hall: the black frame is a perfect cube made out of five identical pieces of bentwood supporting a veneer seat with a rectangular slot for lifting. Soon, chairs in the new "Postsparkassen style" appeared in the Thonet catalogue.

Wagner's Post Office Savings Bank was a *Gesamtkunstwerk*, a total work of art in which architecture, decor, and furnishings contributed to the aesthetic effect. This all-encompassing approach was the foundation of the Wiener Werkstätte, an artists' and craftsmen's cooperative that undertook architectural commissions and produced furniture,

*Postsparkasse stool
(Otto Wagner)*

textiles, tableware, and jewelry and other luxury goods. In 1907, the Werkstätte established its own nightclub, the Cabaret Fledermaus, in the cellar of a Viennese apartment house. The architect Josef Hoffmann, co-founder of the Werkstätte, was not only responsible for the decor, he also designed the furniture, as well as the crockery, silverware, and serving dishes. The nightclub's bentwood chairs had an upholstered seat and a curved unpadded back rail that became the arms. By all accounts the chairs were not particularly comfortable, but they were a radical departure from the bentwood chairs of the past, with runners instead of straight legs and stylish ornament in the form of billiard-ball-size spheres. Kohn supplied the chair in an ebonized finish with white balls, and vice versa. The ball motif also showed up in Hoffman's *Sitzmaschine*, a lounge chair designed in 1905 for another Werkstätte project, the Purkersdorf Sanatorium outside Vienna. The frames that formed the arms, legs, and back of the chair were bent ash; the solid inserts with decorative cutouts were sycamore. The back was adjustable and a footrest pulled out from under the seat. The chair was provided with a fitted cushion, although with its flat back, square geometry, and hard surfaces it doesn't look very inviting. According to the Museum of Modern Art, which has the *Sitzmaschine* in its collection: "This armchair, with its exposed structure, demonstrates a rational simplification of forms suited to machine production." Actually, most of the little wooden balls appear highly *ir*rational, the "simple" connections all rely on screws, and because there are so many different parts to assemble the claim that the form is suited to machine production is far-fetched. On the other hand, it definitely *looks* machinelike.

By the early 1900s, in addition to traditional designs, which constituted the bulk of their production, Gebrüder

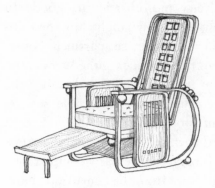

Sitzmaschine
(*Josef Hoffmann*)

Thonet and other bentwood manufacturers were offering "modern" chairs, many of which were designed by architects. The desire of avant-garde architects to furnish interiors with furniture of their own design was not uncommon at the time. M. H. Baillie Scott and C.F.A. Voysey in London, Charles Rennie Mackintosh and his wife, Margaret, in Glasgow, and the young Frank Lloyd Wright in Chicago also designed special chairs. But these architect-designed chairs were custom-made in small quantities in local workshops and were not available to the public, whereas Wagner's bank stool and Hoffmann's *Sitzmaschine* could be purchased from the Thonet and Kohn showrooms.

The Viennese collaboration between architects and industry signals a historical shift. For centuries, the man who conceived the chair and the man who made it had been the same person. This started to change in the eighteenth century: Chippendale was assisted by journeymen joiners, but at least by training and experience he was familiar with the craft. A French master joiner had a similar intimate knowledge of chairmaking, even if the carving, gilding, and upholstery were done by others. By the time Michael Thonet's factories were in full swing, he must be considered more an entrepreneur than a cabinetmaker, although the fabrication process was his own invention and the chairs were his design. By the early 1900s, the industrial process that Thonet invented made it possible to separate the design of a chair from its fabrication. The era of the independent chair designer, who was neither a cabinetmaker nor a manufacturer, had arrived.

EIGHT

By Design

The Wassily Chair is a modern classic. This version of a traditional club chair is made out of leather straps stretched inside a framework of shiny steel tubes. The Vitra Design Museum describes the chair as "the epitome of the spirit of Modernity" and "an aesthetic turning point in furniture production." A Museum of Modern Art catalogue accompanying a recent exhibition on the Bauhaus didn't mince words and simply called it "perfect."

I came across the Wassily Chair as an architecture student. I knew it only from photographs—none of my friends owned one—so I never had a chance to sit in it, but I wanted one. I must have told my wife about my craving, for one year she presented me with the chair on my birthday. It was as handsome in real life as it had been in photographs. The leather seat, back, and arms seemed to be suspended in midair within a metal frame that had the appearance of an early flying machine. I looked forward to using it for reading, but I was disappointed when I sat in it. The extreme angle of the seat allowed only one sitting position, so I soon started to fidget—as much as this unyielding chair would allow. The hard edge of the leather cut into the underside of my thighs; the armrest, which resembled a barber's strop, was unpleasant; getting up was difficult; and when I placed a book on the seat, it slid off. Eventually, the chair was relegated to our bedroom, where it functioned perfectly as a place to hang my trousers.

How is it possible for a chair with so many functional shortcomings to become a classic? The brief answer is that what makes Marcel Breuer's Wassily Chair a classic has less to do with its performance than with its appearance. In other words, the criteria are chiefly aesthetic. "I think that comfort is a function of whether you think the chair is good-looking or not," Philip Johnson once observed. "I have had Mies van der Rohe chairs now for twenty-five years in my home wherever I go. They are not very comfortable chairs, but, if people like the looks of them they say 'Aren't these beautiful chairs,' which indeed they are. Then they'll sit in them and say, 'My, aren't they comfortable.'" Johnson didn't reveal what people said when they tried to get up out of Mies's Barcelona Chairs, which are very low and lack arms. Probably "Oof!"

The idea that a chair can be appreciated primarily as an aesthetic object originated with the Dutch designer Gerrit Rietveld. Although Rietveld was trained as a cabinetmaker by his joiner father, the iconic easy chair that he built in 1918, a year after opening his own furniture workshop in Amsterdam, owed little to the furniture maker's craft. The chair was made out of

Wassily Chair
(Marcel Breuer)

pieces of standard lumber simply screwed together—no dovetails, no mortise-and-tenon joints. The seat and the back were flat wooden planks.

In some ways, Rietveld's chair resembles my trusty Adirondack chair. The Adirondack chair, which was invented by Thomas Lee in 1903, likewise uses flat boards and uncomplicated joints. But the resemblance ends there. Lee's aim was to make a simple outdoor chair for his summer house in Westport, New York; Rietveld's aim was to make an artistic statement. The statement was about geometry and space. Each part of the chair—seat, back, legs, arms—was articulated and given equal visual importance. The wood was initially varnished, but in later versions Rietveld painted the back red, the seat blue, and the frame black and yellow, which made it look like a three-dimensional Mondrian painting (Rietveld and Mondrian both belonged to the De Stijl art group). The chair became known as the Red Blue Chair. The use of a title is revealing. Thonet simply assigned catalogue numbers or descriptive labels to his chairs, but Rietveld's chair was a work of art, so it had to have a title.

The Red Blue Chair abounds with ergonomic challenges: the edges are sharp, the seat is hard and steeply angled, the armrests are flat pieces of wood. According to the architectural historian Peter Collins, Rietveld's chair was "the first chair deliberately designed not for comfort, not for dignity, not for elegance, not for rational assembly according to commonly accepted principles of woodwork, but simply 'designed.'" For the early-twentieth-century European avant-garde, "design" was a universal language, the visual equivalent of Esperanto. The architect Walter Gropius expressed a commonly held view when he proclaimed, "the process of designing a great building or a simple chair differs only in degree, not in principle." According to Collins, not only did modern chairs resemble architectural structures, modern buildings came to resemble furniture, inasmuch as they were designed "to look good from the air: i.e., from the point of view which one normally sees furniture when entering a room."

Gropius founded the Bauhaus arts and crafts school to teach his universalist proposition. One of his first students was a young Hungarian, Marcel Breuer, who had been an art student in Vienna, but dissatisfied with what he considered an overly theoretical education had enrolled in the Bauhaus woodworking program. A precocious talent, Breuer became Gropius's protégé, and after he graduated he was invited back to teach furniture design. That was 1925, and that same year, working in his spare time, Breuer built the Wassily Chair.* He was only twenty-three, and although he had built wooden chairs as a student, this was his first project in tubular steel. The overall form of the chair was influenced by Rietveld's Red Blue Chair, which had been exhibited at the Bauhaus. Like the Red Blue Chair, the Wassily Chair was a constructivist design statement, although it was slightly more inviting because the stretched fabric of the original was more accommodating than flat wood.

Breuer ordered the nickel-plated tubular steel pieces from the Mannessmann Steel Works, which, in the 1890s, had invented a process of manufacturing seamless tubes that, unlike the seamed variety, could be bent. Breuer said that his interest in tubular steel was sparked by the handlebars of his first bicycle. He recalled that a friend told him: "Did you

---

*"Wassily" refers to the painter Wassily Kandinsky, who also taught at the Bauhaus. The name was not coined by Breuer but by an Italian manufacturer in 1960.

ever see how they make those parts? How they bend those handlebars? You would be interested because they bend those steel tubes like macaroni." Although German hospitals used furniture made out of steel, which was more hygienic than wood, no one had previously used tubular steel for a domestic chair.

It is impossible to overstate the impact of Breuer's chair on the architectural avant-garde. The design ethos of the time was "starting over," that is, doing away with traditional forms and traditional ornament. In buildings this meant flat-roofed, undecorated white boxes, but how to start over in furniture? The Red Blue Chair was more like a manifesto than an actual piece of furniture, nor was it really suited to industrial production, despite its maker's claim. Tubular steel, on the other hand, was an industrial product—and looked it. This was the first technical innovation in furniture-making since Michael Thonet developed bentwood sixty-five years earlier.

Breuer was uniquely qualified to lead the way. He had experience, having built furniture for several of Gropius's projects and for Bauhaus exhibitions. He had sufficient expertise in carpentry to pass a journeyman's exam after graduation, but his imagination was not constrained by traditional furniture-making techniques. He belonged to the first generation that was trained in modernist design principles—when Breuer had been a Bauhaus student, the master of the carpentry shop and his teacher was Johannes Itten, the Swiss expressionist painter and radical design theorist.

For Breuer, the five years following the introduction of the Wassily Chair were intensely productive. He designed a variety of furniture for the new Bauhaus buildings: side chairs and sofa beds for the faculty housing, tilt-up theater seats for the auditorium, and tables and stools for the cafeteria—all in tubular steel. The furniture was handmade in the school workshop but Breuer had industrial production in mind; like Thonet, he used standardized parts and designed the chairs to be knocked down for shipping. In 1927, together with Kalman Lengyel, a fellow Hungarian, Breuer founded Standard-Möbel specifically to manufacture and market his own furniture.

Thanks to Lengyel's mismanagement the company foundered, and it was soon acquired by Gebrüder Thonet, which, starting in 1928, took over the manufacture of Breuer's designs. Although tubular steel chairs are often described as lightweight and inexpensive, compared with bentwood they were neither. Steel is heavier than wood (the Wassily Chair weighs thirty pounds, almost twice as much as a typical bentwood lounge chair), and precision tubular steel was expensive: a Breuer side chair cost about three times as much as a typical café chair. Nevertheless, Thonet wanted to diversify, and tubular steel furniture was the perfect opportunity to be in the forefront of the industry once again.

Breuer had noticed that if the Bauhaus cafeteria stool was turned on its side it became, in effect, a seat supported on two legs—a cantilever chair. There had been several earlier attempts to build cantilever chairs. The most serious effort was made by Mart Stam, a Dutch architect living in Berlin, who in 1926 began experimenting with tubular furniture. Stam built a crude cantilever chair out of threaded steel pipes connected by plumbing elbows; the first prototype collapsed when he sat on it, but he persevered. Whether he got the idea after talking to Breuer and seeing his tubular experiments, as Breuer later claimed, or whether he developed the concept independently remains unclear, but there is no doubt that the tubular steel and canvas chair that Stam displayed at the 1927 Weissenhoff Exhibition in Stuttgart is the first successful example of a cantilever chair.

The Weissenhoff housing exhibition, which featured buildings designed by leading avant-garde architects such as Le Corbusier, Walter Gropius, Josef Frank, and Mart Stam, was coordinated by Mies van der Rohe. At an organizational meeting, Stam showed Mies a sketch of his idea for a cantilever chair. Mies recognized the breakthrough that the chair represented and immediately set about designing his own version, which was also displayed at the Stuttgart exhibition. Mies's design is much more elegant than Stam's—the front legs curve into the seat in a sweeping arc—and it also includes a small but crucial difference. Stam used cast tubing and reinforced the bends by inserting pieces of solid steel rod, which created a strong but perfectly rigid frame. Like Breuer, Mies used Mannessmann tubing, which allowed the chair to flex. Such springiness, analogous to the movement of a rocking chair, was something entirely new in sitting furniture.

Although Mies had previously designed wood furniture, the MR10 was his first chair in tubular steel, and it is a reflection of his talent that he was able to produce this beautiful chair in only six months. But he was not experienced in designing for industry. While the MR10 looked extremely simple, it was not easy to fabricate and turned out to be the most expensive tubular chair in Thonet's line. The design had another drawback: like all cantilever chairs, it tended to tip forward if you sat on the edge. Thonet modified the design to lessen the tippiness, but it could not be removed altogether. It's always risky to sit on the edge of a cantilever chair.

A year after Mies produced the MR10, Breuer unveiled

MR10 cantilever chair
(Ludwig Mies van der Rohe)

Cesca Chair
(Marcel Breuer)

his own version of a cantilever side chair. The Wassily Chair
had been a youthful effort that privileged aesthetics over
practicality. Now, although still only twenty-six, Breuer was
an experienced designer and he brought the two into balance with his Cesca Chair, manufactured by Thonet as
B32.* The seat and back are beechwood frames with woven
cane inserts; because the frames are shaped and curved they
are more comfortable than stretched fabric or leather. In addition, the frames act as bracing, reducing the amount of
tubing required. The armchair version (B64) extends the tubular frame to support wooden armrests. Later in Breuer's
career, when he was designing houses, he regularly incorporated traditional materials such as fieldstone and rough slate,
leading Philip Johnson to quip that Breuer was a "peasant
mannerist." The enduring appeal of the Cesca Chair derives
from a similar combination of tradition with innovation,
shaped wood and woven cane with shiny steel. Starting over,
but also looking back.

---

*The chair was named in the 1950s, after Breuer's daughter Francesca.

No. A811F chair
(Josef Frank)

Although the MR10 and the Cesca were acclaimed by modernist architects, tubular steel furniture was not a runaway commercial success. According to Christopher Wilk of the Victoria and Albert Museum, the royalties paid by Thonet to Breuer suggest that "sales may not have amounted to more than a few hundred pieces a year." The 1920s did see an unexpected revival of early Thonet bentwood chairs, thanks largely to their newfound popularity among the architectural avant-garde. Le Corbusier, for example, was a great admirer of bentwood chairs. One of his favorites was the No. B9 *Schreibtischfauteuil*, a writing armchair with a circular seat and arms that curved into the circular backrest. Le Corbusier's work was well publicized, and Thonet's bentwood furniture—much of which was now more than fifty years old—became associated with the radical new architecture.

Le Corbusier did not design any bentwood chairs himself, but another modernist architect did: the Viennese Josef Frank. A friend of Adolf Loos and a protégé of Hoffmann, Frank refined an earlier Thonet chair that had been designed in the mid-1920s by Adolf Gustav Schneck. Schneck had used a single continuous piece of bentwood to form the back as well as the two arms. Frank used the same configuration but replaced the solid seat with woven cane and added a caned backrest. He also eliminated the leg brace and gave the legs a slight flare, resulting in a poised, delicate stance that recalls a cabriole. The No. A811F is the bentwood chair

I had in my university office.* Despite using nineteenth-century techniques, the well-proportioned, squarish form is markedly modern; it is also a very comfortable chair. The simplicity of the design—only six pieces—rivals the classic café chair. Michael Thonet would have approved.

On Bent Knee

Thonet featured No. A811F on the cover of its 1933 catalogue. By then, tubular steel furniture had run its course.† The British writer on design John Gloag considered it a "rather bleak phase of functionalism in design." The novelist Aldous Huxley was more cutting: "Personally I very much dislike the aseptic, hospital style of furnishing. To dine off an operating table, to loll in a dentist's chair—this is not my idea of domestic bliss." Even some modernist architects had doubts. "The tubular steel chair is surely rational from technical and constructive points of view," wrote one. "It is light, suitable for mass production, and so on. But steel and chromium surfaces are not satisfactory from the human point of view."

The man who wrote that was the Finnish architect Alvar Aalto. He had at first been enthusiastic about tubular steel furniture. As early as 1928, he had bought a set of Breuer's furniture—including a Wassily Chair—for his own home, and he used Breuer's cantilever side chairs in a restaurant project. He and his wife, Aino, also an architect, designed a

---

*The A811F is sometimes called the Prague Chair, a name that originated with Charles Stendig, whose company imported the chair to the United States in the 1950s. Stendig credited Josef Hoffmann with the design, although most historians today ascribe it to Frank.

† By the 1930s, Thonet was no longer a leader in chair design. The upheaval of World War II and the subsequent nationalization of Thonet factories behind the Iron Curtain would signal the demise of the company as a global force.

stacking "hybrid chair" that combined a tubular frame with a molded plywood seat. Aalto called it "the world's first soft wooden chair" because it had the characteristic springiness of a cantilever chair. But in time he became dissatisfied with steel furniture. What disturbed him was the very thing that appealed to the "house is a machine for living" architects—the cold, hard, industrial shininess of the material.

Alvar and Aino Aalto set out to design modern furniture using wood instead of tubular steel. The Aaltos were architects, but they approached the problem like cabinetmakers. Emulating Michael Thonet, they began with the fabrication process. The first challenge was the material: Finnish birch is not as flexible as Moravian beechwood, and it can be bent in only one direction, parallel to the grain. Working with a local master joiner, they experimented with different ways of bending, shaping, gluing, and laminating birchwood. The opportunity to apply this knowledge came in 1929 when the Aaltos won a competition to design a tuberculosis sanatorium near Paimio, Finland. They were responsible for the interior design: hardware, lighting fixtures, wardrobes, as well as assorted furniture: tables, waiting room armchairs, reading room chairs, cafeteria side chairs, outdoor reclining chairs, physicians' swivel desk chairs, and laboratory stools. The most original designs were two all-wood lounge chairs that used a single piece of thin curved plywood as a seat, supported by a frame made out of bent veneered birch.* One frame was a cantilever and the other was a closed loop; like the Wassily Chair, both models were supported by runners. All-wood furniture suited a sanatorium, being less noisy

---

*Aalto was influenced by his friend the Swedish architect Erik Gunnar Asplund, who in 1925 had designed an easy chair—the Senna Chair—with a shell-like seat and back of leather stretched on carved walnut.

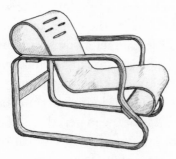

Paimio lounge chair
(Alvar and Aino Aalto)

when moved compared with tubular steel. Aesthetically, the curving wood frames were less machinelike, and the wide wooden frames made for better armrests.

Most of the Paimio furniture made its way into production. The two lounge chairs, the waiting room armchair, and the reading room chair are still being made today by Artek, a company founded by the Aaltos in 1935. We have an Artek barstool in our kitchen. The stool arrived from Finland in a flat carton, six pieces of birchwood: a circular seat covered in black linoleum, four legs, a circular brace that doubles as a footrest, and sixteen screws. The design—which dates from 1935—is not complicated. The legs are bent pieces of solid birch that are simply screwed to the underside of the seat; the circular footrest of laminated birch is similarly attached to the legs. The fourteen-inch-diameter seat is generous, and the legs splay slightly to create more stability. A stool is a utilitarian sort of seat, but this one has attitude.

The key to Aalto's designs was the bent leg. "In furniture design the basic problem from an historical—and practical—point of view is the connecting element between the vertical and horizontal pieces," he wrote. "I believe this is absolutely decisive in giving the style its character." This is apparent in cabriole chairs, Windsor chairs, and bentwood café chairs. Aalto devised an original method of bending solid birch.

The wood was kerfed, that is, thin slots were cut into one end. After the piece was soaked in water and briefly steamed, plywood strips coated with glue were slid into the kerfs. Then the piece was bent to the required angle in a mold. Aalto called the L-shaped leg a "bent knee." It could serve equally well for a chair, a stool, or a table.

Although Aalto designed chairs that are actually more suited to mass production than many of their tubular steel cousins, he abhorred standardization, which he called "industrial violence against individual taste." What makes his chairs so appealing is that while they are factory-made objects and use standardized components, they don't look standardized. They are not handcrafted, yet they somehow carry a human imprint. The plywood is generally painted, but solid wood is always coated with clear lacquer so the grain of the pale birch comes through. The shapes have more to do with the world of nature than with abstract geometry. "There are only two things in art," said Aalto, "humanity or its lack." That conviction comes through, too.

Alakazam!

Aalto's bentwood chairs found an international market. In 1933, an assortment of Aalto furniture was displayed as part of an exhibition of Finnish furniture at the fashionable London department store Fortnum & Mason. The leading British journal *Architectural Review* sponsored the show and published an enthusiastic article on Aino and Alvar Aalto's chairs, which it called "cheap and seemly furniture which is comfortable, light and easy to move." The Aalto display included the plywood-and-tubular-steel side chair, several lounge chairs, and a stack of stools. The unpretentious furniture appealed to those with modern tastes and soon led to foreign orders for the newly founded Artek. The Paimio waiting room armchair was marketed in Britain as the Verandah Chair. The appeal of all-wood furniture was not lost on other designers, including Breuer, who designed a series of molded plywood lounge chairs for the British manufacturer Isokon.

Another designer who was influenced by Aalto was the young Eero Saarinen, son of Eliel Saarinen, a celebrated architect and the head of the Cranbrook Academy of Art in Bloomfield Hills, Michigan. Born in Finland and brought to America as a boy, Eero was groomed by his father to be an architect. In 1935, after graduating from Yale's school of architecture, the young Eero spent a year working in Helsinki, where, because Aalto was a family friend, he became familiar with Artek's innovative wood furniture. Aalto's influence is evident in a chair that Eero designed immediately after joining his father's architectural firm. Eliel was designing the Kleinhans Music Hall in Buffalo, and Eero was responsible for the armchairs that constituted the auditorium seating. The design is clearly based on Aalto's Paimio waiting room chair: the seat and back, which are covered by a thin padding and cotton upholstery, are a single piece of molded plywood supported by a rectangular maple frame.

Eero Saarinen worked on the Kleinhans chair with his friend Charlie—Charles Eames. A few years older than Saarinen, Eames had dropped out of architecture school in St. Louis, apprenticed with a local architect, and eventually opened his own office. One of his houses so impressed Eliel Saarinen that he offered the thirty-one-year-old architect a fellowship to Cranbrook. Architectural commissions in post-Depression America being scarce, Eames accepted. Thanks to his evident abilities and experience, after only a

*Reading chair
(Eero Saarinen and
Charles Eames)*

year he was put in charge of Cranbrook's industrial design department. In his spare time he worked
in the Saarinen office.

Eames and Eero Saarinen became
fast friends—and collaborators. In
1940, the Museum of Modern Art
announced an inter-American furniture design competition—"Organic
Design in Home Furnishings"—
which they entered together. They
decided that the logical development
of the Kleinhans chair would be a
chair made of plywood molded in *three* dimensions. In a remarkable creative effort, the pair produced a reading chair, a
side chair, a high-back armchair, and a lounge chair. All dispensed with supporting frames and used plywood shells in
which the seat, back, and arms were made of one continuous
material. Saarinen and Eames had intended to leave the plywood shell exposed, but the quality of the finish was poor so
they covered the plywood with foam rubber and fabric. The
legs were to be metal, but, pressed for time, the designers
made them birch. The jury, which included Marcel Breuer
and Alvar Aalto, awarded the shell chairs first prize.

The Saarinen-Eames chairs were not commercially produced, partly because of the outbreak of World War II, and
partly because their cost was prohibitive due to the complicated geometry.* Nevertheless, no one who saw the chairs
in the Museum of Modern Art, or in the twelve major department stores across the country where they were also

---

*When the Saarinen-Eames chair was finally put into production (in 2004), the
price of the reading chair exceeded $2,000.

displayed, would ever think of a chair in quite the same way again.

Wartime marked the end of the partnership. Saarinen stayed in Michigan to work with his father, and Eames, now married, moved to Los Angeles. He and his wife, Ray, who had been a student at Cranbrook, continued experimenting with molding plywood. Like Alvar and Aino Aalto, they focused on the fabrication method. They built a homemade molding machine into which cardboard-thin layers of plywood, slathered with glue, were placed. A bladder inflated by a hand-operated car tire pump pressed the plies into a plaster mold, and heating elements bonded the glue. After four to six hours, the mold was opened, and—alakazam—a piece of molded plywood magically emerged. They called their contraption the Kazam! machine.

The Eameses' first molded plywood product was a leg splint for the U.S. Navy; by the end of the war they had fabricated 150,000 of them. They also worked on molded plywood medical litters and fuselage parts for gliders. This practical experience led to a postwar line of children's furniture and large children's toys. But their goal remained an industrially produced chair, as Charles later explained:

> The idea was to do a piece of furniture that would be simple and yet comfortable. It would be a chair on which mass production would not have anything but a positive influence; it would have in its appearance the essence of the method that produced it. It would have an inherent rightness about it, and it would be produced by people working in a dignified way. That sounds a little pompous, but at the time it was a perfectly legitimate thing to strive for.

Dining Chair Metal
(Charles and Ray Eames)

The first prototypes of a molded shell chair were made in 1945. The shells were produced on an improved version of the Kazam! machine; the entire process now took only ten minutes. The seat and the back were two separate pieces of molded plywood—five plies of ash, a total of 5/16 inch thick—supported by a frame of extremely thin steel rods. The plywood was connected to the frame by rubber shock mounts that were electrostatically welded to the wood using an innovative process developed by the Chrysler Corporation. The rubber mounts gave the chair some resilience; there was no padding or upholstery. The molded plywood back and seat seemed to float above the skinny metal frame, giving rise to the nickname "potato-chip chair." There were two versions, a side chair and a lounge chair; the latter was two inches lower, with a slightly larger seat and a more reclined back. The pragmatic Charles called them DCM and LCM (Dining Chair Metal and Lounge Chair Metal). A second version of the chairs substituted molded plywood for the steel frame.

The Herman Miller company of Zeeland, Michigan, began manufacturing the Eames chairs in 1946. The chairs were a success—artistically and commercially. They were endorsed by the Museum of Modern Art, and by 1951, the DCM, which was by far the most popular model, was selling at the rate of two thousand a month. A 1952 magazine advertisement in *House & Garden* announced: "America's Most Famous Modern Chair Can Now be Yours For $25." The potato-chip chair has proven a remarkably durable design. When Renzo Piano designed the New York Times Building in 2007, he furnished the cafeteria with DCMs. I'm not sure which is more remarkable: that he picked a sixty-year-old furniture design for the new building, or that the chairs still look fresh and up-to-date.

Because the Eames plywood chair is molded in three dimensions it provides the same comfort as the hand-carved seat of a Windsor chair. At the same time, it is a beautiful object. Charles Eames was once asked if furniture design was an expression of art. "The design is an expression of the purpose," he answered. "It may (if it is good enough) later be judged as art." Ray Eames was trained as an artist, and many people saw her hand in the sculptural shapes. Arthur Drexler, then curator of architecture and design at the Museum of Modern Art, observed: "Ambiguous but not bland, the shape is instantly seen as a whole, with no part of its contour catching the eye. The curve of the seat flares more emphatically and from certain angles gives the chair a curiously animated look." If Drexler's last phrase sounds tentative it is because modern design was supposed to be abstract, but what makes the Eames chair so endearing—especially the version with insectlike metal legs—is that it appears as zoomorphic, in its own whimsical way, as a cabriole chair.

Charles and Ray Eames separated the seat and back of the plywood chair in order to simplify the molding process. But a one-piece shell, which Eames and Saarinen had explored earlier, remained the goal. After experimenting with stamped steel and aluminum, which proved too expensive, the Eameses turned to plastic. Polyester resin reinforced with fiberglass cloth had been developed by Owens-Corning in the late 1930s and had come into its own in aircraft production during the war. Some of the earliest nonmilitary

Plastic shell armchair
(Charles and Ray Eames)

fiberglass products were sailing dinghies, and a hydraulic press adapted from the boatbuilding industry was used to manufacture the first Eames chairs. The shell came in three colors—gray, beige, and parchment (later, brighter colors were introduced, as well as fabric and vinyl upholstery). The shell was attached with rubber shock mounts to a variety of bases: wire struts; tubular metal or wood legs; swivel pedestals with casters; even wooden rockers. There were two versions—a side chair and an armchair. In time, the ubiquitous shells were adapted to barstools, stacking classroom chairs, and auditorium and stadium seating.

The Eames shell chair—the world's first plastic chair—was even more revolutionary than the potato-chip chair, because it was not simply the result of an innovative manufacturing technique, like bending wood or tubular steel, but also used a new material. A decade later, the British chair designer Robin Day produced a shell chair molded out of polypropylene, the Polyprop Chair.* While not as elegant as the Eames design, it was considerably less expensive, the modern equivalent of the Thonet café chair—"the price of a bottle of good wine." The ultimate descendant of the Eames shell chair is the ubiquitous one-piece plastic chair that will be discussed in the final chapter.

The year that the Eames shell chair appeared—1950—*Life* published an article on Charles Eames that called him "the best-known U.S. designer of modern furniture," which

---

*Today, Eames shell chairs are also made of injection-molded polypropylene.

was true although it ignored Ray's contribution. "Eames is
so interested in making the products of his drawing board
available at the lowest cost that the modest retail price of his
recent chair ($32.50) bothers him . . . he guiltily feels that it
should sell for less." Four plastic Eames chairs cost $130 at a
time when a chrome kitchen dinette set of four chairs *and*
a table sold for well under a hundred dollars. My parents
had one of these sets in the kitchen when I was growing up
in the 1950s: the tabletop was Formica in a cracked-ice pattern, the chairs had shiny tubular steel frames with seats and
backs upholstered in marbled vinyl. They were pretty clumsy
compared with the graceful Eames chairs.

Charles and Ray Eames designed many more chairs: a
wire mesh version of the shell chair; a luxurious, extremely
popular lounge chair and ottoman that combined plywood
shells with deep leather upholstery; and a line of cast-aluminum
office furniture that used thin padded slings as seats and
backs. In the 1960s, the Eameses produced a variety of expensive executive office chairs, but it was the plastic chair that
remained closest to their goal of a chair that was "simple
and yet comfortable" with "an inherent rightness." Eames
had nothing to feel guilty about—he had achieved what
many modern chair designers strove for but few attained.

Fewer than twenty-five years separate the Eames plastic
shell chair from Marcel Breuer's first cantilever chair. Both
share an iconoclastic approach, using new materials in novel
ways. Both chairs are loosely referred to as "modern," and
both are dramatic departures from convention. Breuer's cantilever chair is actually more radical, since it is a chair on
only two legs and incorporates an unprecedented springiness. In that regard, the Eames shell chair is more traditional: a seat supported by four legs. However, appearances
can be deceiving. The Breuer chair, although it embodies the

image of a machine-made object, is a crafted artifact largely assembled by hand, while the Eames chair is a true industrial product.* Yet the latter would not exist without the former. Breuer set the agenda—a chair that would be manufactured rather than built, and whose appearance would be the result of how it was made. The Eames shell chair fulfilled this ambitious goal.

The Cesca Chair, the Paimio lounge chair, the potato-chip chair, and the plastic shell chair are true modern classics. They fulfill the ideal of combining new processes and new materials to produce new forms. The forms are not simply aesthetic inventions; they are the result of considerable technical innovation and refinement. There have been many unusually shaped chairs since, but few real rivals, which is probably why all four chairs remain in production today. Like the cabriole chair and the bentwood chair, they represent an enduring kind of perfection, a considered balance between means and ends.

---

*This explains why today the Cesca costs more than twice as much as an Eames shell chair.

NINE

Great Dane

"It was not until about sixty years ago that the ultimate test of architectural genius became whether or not one could design a new kind of chair," observed Peter Collins. He wrote that in 1963, and since then the number of architects designing chairs has multiplied. A recent example is the Dream Chair, the work of the prizewinning Japanese architect Tadao Ando, who had never designed a production chair before. I thought it would be interesting to see the chair—and to sit on it.

The Dream Chair is prominently displayed in the New York showroom of Carl Hansen & Søn, an established Danish furniture manufacturer. This lounge chair is made out of two large molded plywood shells, one for the seat and the other for the base. "It is possible with standard plywood to have minor double-curved planes, but it will for sure not be possible to bend the Ando chair with normal veneer," explained Jesper Bruun, Hansen's head of development, in an e-mail. He described the unconventional veneer of the Dream Chair as "wooden strings held together by glue."

The chair is punctuated by three ovals: a padded headrest,

a hole cut into the seat, and an identical hole in the base. The headrest is adjustable, a ratcheted feature commonly found in car seats but which strikes me as slightly out of place in a domestic chair. The base is cantilevered, so that when I sit down the chair flexes pleasantly. However, after a few minutes, the edge of the hole that is cut into the seat also cuts into my tail bone. It is a small but persistent irritant, like having a tiny stone in one's shoe.

Looking around the Hansen showroom I recognize another plywood chair, an older model originally introduced more than fifty years ago. A low easy chair, it also consists of two pieces of curved plywood—a seat and back. They are supported on three legs: the two front legs made out of a single curved piece of laminated wood, and a hind leg doubling as a support for the backrest. Upholstered pads are attached to the plywood with brass fasteners that are plainly visible on the back and underside. My first impression is of an improbable tour de force: four pieces of wood, three legs, swooping curves. But when I sit down, I appreciate the roomy proportions and the comfortable shape. The sculptural "wings" that flare out dramatically on each side are actually convenient places to rest my hands—and to push against when I get up. The designer, Hans Wegner, had two decades of experience under his belt when he designed this chair, and it shows.

Wegner "helped change the course of design history in the 1950s and '60s by sanding modernism's sharp edges and giving aesthetes a comfortable seat," read his *New York Times* obituary. In *The Shape of Time*, George Kubler pointed out that the impact of an artist depends not only on his personal abilities but also on the timing of his entrance onto the world stage. "Each man's lifework is also a work in a series extending beyond him in either or both directions,

Shell Chair (Hans Wegner)

depending upon his position in the track he occupies," he wrote. Wegner's position in the track of furniture history was particularly fortuitous: he was in the right place at exactly the right moment.

Hans J. Wegner was born in 1914 in Tønder, a small town in southern Denmark. He grew up in a craft tradition; his father was a master cobbler. At fourteen, young Hans was apprenticed to a local cabinetmaker—his qualifying project for the journeyman's exam was a lady's desk. When he was twenty-one, he went to Copenhagen to fulfill his military service. The city opened his eyes, and he realized that his knowledge of furniture design—as opposed to joinery—was limited. The following year, after completing a short cabinetmaker's course he enrolled in the Cabinetmaker Day School. The Day School was an offshoot of the furniture school of the Royal Danish Academy of Fine Arts, whose founder and director was Kaare Klint, an architect and cabinetmaker who is sometimes called the godfather of modern Danish furniture.

Klint, who was born in 1888, considered the chair a functional necessity—a tool for sitting—but while he was no historicist, he did not reject the past. "All the problems are not new, and several of them have been solved before," he instructed his students. His own designs were often updated versions of traditional chairs, especially English chairs, which he particularly admired. His oeuvre included a wing chair, a leather-covered club chair, a deep leather love seat, a chaise longue based on a steamer chair, and a rush-bottomed church chair of Shaker-like simplicity. Klint pioneered the teaching of anthropometrics—the study of body measurements—in chair design. He also emphasized the importance of details, which would become a leading characteristic of Danish furniture.

Klint's lifetime output of chairs, tables, and cabinets amounted to only thirty pieces. There is a story that he was once visited by a friend, the Swedish architect Erik Gunnar Asplund, who described his current projects, and Klint responded that he was designing a chair. The two met again a couple of years later, and after Asplund described several new commissions he asked Klint what he was up to. "Well, I told you the last time we met," he replied with what sounds like exasperation, "I am working on a chair." That particular chair came to be known as the Red Chair, thanks to the color of its oxhide upholstery. It is a mahogany side chair, with delicately curved and splayed rear legs and the proportions of a Chippendale cabriole chair, although there are no decorations and the inviting concave front rail of the seat is not a Chippendale detail.

The much-admired Red Chair won a grand prix medal at the 1929 International Exposition in Barcelona, the same event at which Mies van der Rohe unveiled the Barcelona Chair. Klint and Mies shared a modernist sensibility, but not much else. What set the Dane apart from his Bauhaus contemporaries was his devotion to traditional woodworking techniques, and a preference for adapting and distilling rather than inventing. He combined Danish conservatism with a strictly functionalist approach, establishing normative dimensions for furniture, paying close attention to ergonomic comfort, taking care with details, and respecting traditional skills. Above all, he married modern design to old-fashioned craftsmanship.

Unlike many of his friends, Wegner did not apply to the Academy to study under Klint but left the Day School after completing only two years of the three-year course. One has the sense that at twenty-five he was eager to get started. His first job was in the office of the architects Arne Jacobsen and Erik Møller, where he worked on furniture. Jacobsen and Møller were Denmark's leading modernists, and Wegner's designs were simple and undecorated, but they were also rooted in tradition: spindle-back Windsor chairs for the reading room of a library, and distinctly conservative mahogany-and-leather armchairs for the council chamber of a city hall. In the early 1940s, even as Denmark was still under Nazi occupation, Wegner began to work on his own, not as a cabinetmaker but as an independent furniture designer.

Denmark is a small country—in 1940 its population was fewer than 4 million, the economy was still primarily agricultural, and industrialization had barely begun. Furniture was not produced in factories but in small workshops staffed by cabinetmakers and joiners who used traditional woodworking tools and techniques. Danish furniture designers generally collaborated with these workshops, and Wegner established a relationship with the master cabinetmaker Johannes Hansen (no relation to Carl Hansen). One of their first projects—in 1944—was a rocking chair. Its high back and woven seat recall a rush-bottom Shaker rocker, except that instead of a ladder back it had tapered spindles, as slender as those of an American Windsor chair. The rockers of a rocking chair must be slightly splayed, for if they are parallel the rocking movement will cause the chair to creep across the floor. Wegner increased the angle and made the proportions of the seat more generous, like a wedge-shaped cabriole chair. The seat was handwoven three-ply twisted

paper cord.* The four-panel weaving was a traditional technique that
produced a pleasantly shaped seat.
The chair proved extremely popular
and remains in production today.

The crest rail of Wegner's rocking chair is tall enough to support
the head; I know because this is the
chair I sit on when I watch television. This chair affords me great
pleasure, not only because it is comfortable but also because it *feels*
good. The woven seat has a pleas-

Rocking chair
(Hans Wegner)

ant resilience, the arms are slightly curved and rounded, and
the turned pieces have bulging shapes that I can't help
stroking. The beechwood has a clear lacquer finish that allows the wood grain to come through.

In 1947, three years after designing the rather conservative
rocker, Wegner and Hansen's foreman, Nils Thomsen, produced an unusual lounge chair. The exaggerated hoop-back
and slender spindles were obviously influenced by the sack-
back Windsor chair, although the seat was woven cord
rather than solid wood, and the chair was much lower, making for more relaxed sitting. It was a wonderful chair to look
at, and equally wonderful to sit on. Part of the comfort was
the result of the round spindles being flattened at the precise
points where one's shoulders touched the wood. The flattened portions produced a decorative pattern similar to the
eyes of a peacock's tail, which led one of Wegner's colleagues

---

*Twisted paper reinforced with wire was developed in the early 1900s in the
United States to manufacture wicker furniture. Unreinforced paper cord, stronger and longer-lasting than bulrush, was used by so many Danish furniture
makers in the 1940s and '50s that it is often referred to as "Danish cord."

Peacock Chair
(Hans Wegner)

to christen it the Peacock Chair.*
The striking Peacock Chair brought
Wegner instant acclaim and marked
him as an original talent. Its combination of practicality and lavishness
is at odds with Kaare Klint's strait-
laced functionalism. Instead, the
Peacock Chair manages to be cleanly
modern, resolutely old-fashioned, and
glamorous, all at the same time.

Wegner's chairs were the result
of careful study. After exploring an
idea in sketch form, he would make
a 1:5 scale model, as much as possible using the actual materials of the finished product; for example, making the frames
of wood and weaving the cord seats out of string. The models, which are about eight inches high, look remarkably real-
istic in photographs. Next, a full-size prototype would be
built by a cabinetmaker to test construction details and sitting comfort. The final design was recorded by Wegner in a
full-size drawing in which views of the entire chair—side,
front, and top—were shown overlapping on a single sheet.

The use of models and mock-ups recalls the cabinetmakers and *ébénistes* of the eighteenth century. Wegner saw no
contradiction between the demands of industrialization and
the furniture maker's traditional craft. The distinction between design and workmanship was highlighted by the British
design theorist (and accomplished woodworker) David Pye:
"Design is what, for practical purposes, can be conveyed in

---

*Wegner did not name his chairs. The names came either from manufacturers
or from the media. The Peacock Chair was named by the furniture maker Finn
Juhl.

words and by drawing: workmanship is what, for practical purposes, can not." In Wegner's chairs, the two are given equal weight. The design idea is usually apparent first, but the workmanship creeps up on you after you sit down: the tight weave of the paper cord, the smooth shaping of the arms, the subtle taper of a spindle.

The Round One

To encourage innovation and stimulate sales, the 350-year-old Copenhagen Cabinetmakers Guild held an annual exhibition that introduced new works to the public. The exhibition of 1949 featured a number of chairs that used molded plywood. Thanks to the well-publicized success of the Eames potato-chip chair, molded plywood was the material of the moment. Børge Mogensen, who had been Klint's assistant, and was a friend and sometime collaborator of Wegner, showed a plywood chair with teardrop-shaped cutouts. An armchair designed by Bender Madsen and Ejner Larsen, likewise Klint's students, used one piece of shaped plywood to form the back and arms. Jacob Kjær, a cabinetmaker, made an armchair that incorporated a leather-covered plywood seat and back, and Birthe and Torsten Johansson designed an armchair that combined molded teak plywood with an oak frame. Finn Juhl, the most flamboyant of the Danish designers, unveiled a side chair and an armchair—portentously named the Egyptian Chair and the Chieftain's Chair—that combined molded plywood with teak and walnut in dramatic fashion.

Not to be outdone, Wegner and Hansen also entered a molded plywood chair. Wegner had visited the Isokon factory in England, which manufactured Breuer's plywood furniture. Hansen was loathe to invest in the equipment required to mold three-dimensional shells, so Wegner used plywood shells that were bent in only two dimensions. The three shells—seat, back, and headrest—were supported on a bent-wood frame. The commodious chair was unusual—more reclined than a lounge chair, but more vertical than a chaise longue.* A loose sheepskin covered the seat. High tooling costs prevented the three-shell chair from going into production, and it would be another fourteen years before Wegner had the opportunity to design the shell chair that I saw in the New York showroom.

The Hansen-Wegner booth in the 1949 exhibition included an unobtrusive armchair that the designer referred to as "the round one." It had been something of an after-thought. Hansen, who served as president of the cabinetmak-ers' guild, thought that there were too many plywood chairs in the exhibition, and at the last minute he asked Wegner if he had any designs for a more traditional chair. "What do you do when you want to make something typically Dan-ish?" Wegner later recalled. "First, there is oak; oak is typi-cally Danish. Then there's the construction; four equal legs assembled with four frames held together at the top by a wreath." The wreathlike continuous top rail was similar to the bow of a traditional low-back Windsor chair, but shaped like a propellor blade, horizontal armrests morphing into a vertical back support. Using native oak was unusual at a time when most Danish designers favored tropical woods such as Cuban mahogany, Brazilian rosewood, and espe-cially teak. Wegner gave the oak a vegetable-based soaped finish that left the surface looking almost like raw wood. The seat was woven cane. The minimal design fulfilled the

---

*Wegner's three-shell chair anticipated the Eames lounge chair by seven years.

modernist dictum "Form follows function" without appearing in any way industrial.

Round chair with padded seat (Hans Wegner)

The 1949 Copenhagen exhibition was attended by the foreign press for the first time. The following year, *Interiors*, an influential American magazine for architects and interior designers, included an article on the exhibition, which was the first coverage of modern Danish furniture in the American media. No fewer than three of the six pages were devoted to Wegner's work. The article led off with the three-shell chair, and gave pride of place—a full-page photograph—to the round chair. "The sturdy legs are tapered just enough to seem muscular rather than overfed, and the seat dips slightly to look willing but not seductive," read the caption.

The *Interiors* article brought Danish furniture—and Wegner—international recognition. Shortly after the article appeared, he had a visit from a group of Chicago businessmen who were interested in the round chair for their downtown club. Wegner recalled the incident:

> The Americans came to Denmark to inquire whether they could buy or make some of them. Johannes Hansen's workshop was small, with only five or six assistants. They were not used to producing large numbers. If they could just sell the four chairs we made for the show, we would be happy. The Americans were not satisfied with that. They asked if they could get four hundred of them. I could certainly also ask Fritz Hansen [a large furniture maker]—and I did—

but Johannes Hansen certainly didn't like that. The Americans wanted to make the chair in the United States. And I didn't like that. It was designed for Danish craftsmen.

Eventually an agreement was reached and two years later the order was filled. But production remained—and remains today—in Denmark. Wegner was used to having personal oversight of the fabrication process, and the round chair, despite its visual simplicity, is not easy to manufacture. For example, the top rail is formed of three separate pieces of oak cut from the same plank so the grain matches. All the joints are mortised and tenoned, and although the separate parts are today milled and turned on automated machines, they require hand assembly, shaping, and sanding. The round chair remains one of Wegner's more expensive chairs.

Shortly after the 1949 exhibition, Wegner was approached by Carl Hansen & Søn with a request for a dining chair that was similar to the round chair but more suited to mass production. Wegner had seen an illustration of a traditional Chinese folding chair in which the rear legs bent forward to carry the top rail, and he incorporated that feature, which simplified the construction; in addition he shortened the arms to facilitate sitting at the table. The top rail was steam-bent beech; the seat was woven paper cord. The result was more rustic than the sophisticated round chair, although with a distinctive "Oriental" character thanks to the Y-shaped splat. The Y shape was

Wishbone Chair
(Hans Wegner)

not arbitrary; it accommodated the sitter's spine and gave extra support to the top rail. What came to be known as the Wishbone Chair turned out to be Wegner's bestselling chair.

Wegner designed the Wishbone Chair with factory production in mind. The fourteen pieces of wood were turned and milled by machine, and only three of them required steam-bending. On the other hand, it took a craftsman one hour to weave the four hundred feet of paper cord into a seat, and much of the finishing was done by hand. This combination of machine production and handwork—design *and* workmanship—has been called "industrialized craftsmanship." In fact, most of the early modernist chairs by Breuer and Mies also required a great deal of handwork. "If you knew how much polishing work goes into making a Barcelona Chair, you wouldn't call it an industrially made chair," Wegner once wryly remarked. But the handwork in Wegner's chairs—woven cord and scarfed joints—was not remedial; it was intentional and carefully integrated with factory work. The combination proved to be remarkably efficient. The price of a "crafted" Wishbone Chair today is competitive with other modern classics: it costs about the same as an Eames potato-chip chair, and considerably less than a Breuer Cesca or a Mies MR10. "I have always wanted to make unexceptional things of an exceptionally high quality that ordinary people could afford," said Wegner. With the Wishbone Chair, he succeeded.

Industrialized craftsmanship was peculiarly Danish. It was a function of a strong woodworking tradition, the survival of the guild system, and the existence of educational institutions such as the Royal Danish Academy and the Cabinetmaker Day School. Its most important feature was the close collaboration between designers and cabinetmakers.

Ant Chair
(Arne Jacobsen)

The *Interiors* article commented on this arrangement: "The key figures of large American companies—industrial designers or stylists, adapters and efficiency experts, factory workers and industrial craftsmen—do not enter the picture." For a small country, Denmark had an impressive number of exceptional furniture designers. Among the older generation was Kaare Klint, of course; Mogens Koch, who designed a classic folding chair that resembles a director's chair; and Ole Wanscher, whose Egyptian Stool was modeled on the ancient folding stool. Wegner's contemporaries included Børge Mogensen and Finn Juhl. Younger designers such as Verner Panton and Poul Kjærholm were moving away from craft-based production toward industrial materials and manufacturing processes.

It was a member of the older generation who made a major breakthrough in molding plywood. In 1952, Arne Jacobsen, needing a stacking chair for the workers' canteen of a pharmaceutical headquarters, and inspired by the Eames molded plywood chair, designed a light three-legged side chair. The legs were steel tubes, but the seat and back were made out of a single piece of molded plywood—the Holy Grail of chair design. Jacobsen used nine extremely thin veneers and added an inner cotton layer to provide additional reinforcement. Like the Eames DCM chair, the Ant Chair had an insectlike silhouette. Four years later, it was followed by a four-legged version—the Series 7 chair. The Fritz Hansen company, with whom Jacobsen developed the chairs, produced the Series 7 in several versions: various wood veneers;

lacquered, painted, and upholstered; with arms; as a barstool; and as a secretarial chair on casters. The chair flexes pleasantly when you sit on it. My first commission as a young architect was an office interior for a Montreal distributor of high-end cosmetics. I wasn't knowledegable about interior design, but the Series 7 chair—already more than a decade old—caught my fancy. I used it throughout: secretarial chairs, oak veneer chairs in the conference room, and upholstered armchairs in the executive office. The two chairs in the reception area were mustard-colored Ant Chairs. I bought an oak veneer Series 7 for myself. That and a pair of Aalto stools were my first designer chairs.

Danish Modern

The Vitra Design Museum in Weil am Rhein has compiled a list of "100 Masterpieces" of the late nineteenth and twentieth centuries from its collection. The Ant Chair is there; so are Thonet's café chair, Hoffmann's *Sitzmaschine*, and Rietveld's Red Blue Chair. There are two chairs by Mies, two by Aalto, three by Breuer, and six by the Eameses. Wegner earns only one entry, the three-legged shell chair, a very good chair but hardly his most representative design. Moreover, the model in the Vitra collection is an early version, without seating pads and finished in bright red varnish. One senses that this is an attempt to characterize Wegner as "innovative" and "sculptural," the sine qua non of modernist chair design. The truth is that Wegner's work fits awkwardly in the modernist canon. He was innovative when he had to be, but his work was not driven by innovation, and while the shell chair undoubtedly has plastic qualities, most of his chairs look like chairs, not sculptures.

Wegner's approach to design was a result of his tempera-
ment and background—a contemporary described him as
"the most gifted carpenter the world has ever known"—but
he was also a man of his time. He benefitted from the Danish
woodworking tradition without being hobbled by it, and
he built on the foundation established by Kaare Klint
without being merely a disciple. And his work suited the
postwar zeitgeist. The American public especially was
ready—eager, in fact—for something new. In the prosperous 1950s, innovation was in the air, changing the way that
people traveled, worked, played—and lived. The open plan
of the popular one-story ranch house encouraged a more casual lifestyle that called for lighter, simpler furniture. At the
same time, the somewhat clinical designs of orthodox Bauhaus modernism had limited appeal. Wegner's furniture
leavened modernity with craftsmanship, combined simple,
undecorated forms with the tactile pleasure of natural materials, and did not sacrifice the traditional virtues of good
furniture: comfort and utility.

Wegner was part of what became known as the Danish
Modern design movement. Danish Modern included a variety
of domestic products in addition to furniture: printed fabrics, pleated paper lamps, turned teak bowls, stainless-steel
tableware, sterling silver coffee pots. A big part of the appeal
was the integration of art, craft, and industrial design, all dem-
onstrating a consistently humanist sensibility. Danish brands
such as Fritz Hansen, Louis Poulsen, Royal Copenhagen,
and Georg Jensen were recognized internationally. A 1959
photograph taken in Georg Jensen's Manhattan showroom
on the occasion of a retrospective exhibition of Wegner's
furniture shows Wegner and Charles Eames seated in
Wegner-designed chairs. The Dane is explaining something
in an animated fashion, and Eames, dapper in a bow tie, is

listening intently. The subject of their conversation has not been recorded, but what else could it be? Chairs.

The following year, the Metropolitan Museum held an exhibition titled "The Arts of Denmark." Although the wide-ranging displays—designed by Finn Juhl—covered historical periods from the Vikings to the nineteenth century, *The New York Times* declared that the "star of the show" was contemporary Danish design. In passing, the reviewer referred to the "short but happy reign of 'Danish Modern,'" for it was already evident that the popularity of the style was waning. Rising labor costs had made "industrialized craftsmanship" expensive and had led to cheap knockoffs that lacked the originals' quality and attention to detail. Moreover, the period saw the rise of a brittle Pop Art sensibility that favored plastics, geometrical forms, and bright colors, and made soap-treated oak and woven paper cord seem downright quaint. In a word, fashion had changed. An indicator of the depth of the change was that in 1966 the four-decades-old Copenhagen Cabinetmakers Guild exhibition finally closed. An era had ended.

Hans Wegner did not stop designing furniture. He worked with smaller furniture makers such as PP Møbler, which catered to a select clientele. By the time Wegner retired in 1993 (he died in 2007), he had designed more than five hundred chairs, ranging from the quixotic Valet Chair to everyday armchairs for the Danish ferry system, from stools to upholstered sofas. The three-shell lounge chair led to a series of commodious easy chairs that reflected his growing conviction that sitting comfort over extended periods of time required freedom of movement and the ability to change positions. Wegner favored a relaxed posture halfway between sitting and reclining. The story is that he had the idea on a beach, while making himself comfortable in a bowl-

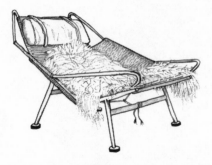

Flag Halyard Chair
(Hans Wegner)

shaped depression in the sand. This insight resulted in one of his most unusual designs, a generous lounge chair that used eight hundred feet of halyard, or nautical rigging line, stretched—not woven—on a tubular stainless-steel frame. The uncharacteristically industrial image of the chrome-plated and painted steel was softened by the natural flax line, a colorful canvas headrest, and a loose, long-haired Icelandic sheepskin. There is nothing minimal or ascetic about this chair, which is luxurious, theatrical, and sybaritic, not traits usually associated with modern design. It also shares a quality with all of Wegner's creations: it is inviting. "A chair is only finished when someone sits in it," he once said.

TEN

Fold and Knockdown, Swing and Roll

Hans Wegner designed several folding chairs that resemble steamer chairs although they are meant for indoor use. The Fireplace Chair—a wood frame with woven leather—supports a fully reclined posture, folds flat, and can be hung on the wall when not in use (it is intended for apartment dwellers). In another folding chair, the rear legs are on wheels, which allows the chair to be trundled around like a wheelbarrow. The best-known—and most copied—Wegner folding chair is a sort of collapsible Barcelona Chair, a low lounge chair of oak and woven cane. It even has handles, to assist in hanging it on the wall.

Chairs have always been associated with mobility. The idea of a portable, part-time seat dates back to the Egyptian folding stool and recurs throughout history: the Scandinavian folding stool, the Cretan camp stool, the Roman curule, the medieval faldstool, the Renaissance scissors chair. The pinned X-frame is the basis for all these chairs, as it is for deck chairs, director's chairs, and Wegner's folding chairs.

The X-frame folding chair can be sat on so the fabric is slung either side-to-side or front-to-back. The ancient

Egyptians, the Greeks, and the Etruscans used front-to-back. The Romans followed this practice, although when they developed the curule, they effectively turned the chair ninety degrees so that the fabric was stretched side-to-side, which influenced the faldstool, the scissors chairs, and the modern camp stool. When the Chinese adopted the folding stool—the "barbarian bed"—they used the Egyptian sitting mode, front-to-back. In the tenth century, when chair-sitting took hold in China, a back and armrests were added, turning the stool into a folding chair—the *jiaoyi*.* The two front legs of the *jiaoyi* curved up to support a horseshoe-shaped back rail, which extended forward to form armrests, an original design that was considerably more sophisticated than any chair found in Europe at the time. Although the sinuous curves anticipate the bentwood chair, the wood was not steam-bent but carved—the back rail consisted of several pieces, the joints reinforced by metal bands. The back rail was further supported by an S-shaped splat, and the seat itself was either woven rope or a solid mat. Ceremonial versions were slightly taller with an attached footrest.

Judging from scroll paintings, Chinese folding chairs were used indoors as well as outside. Unlike the folding stool, which was a utilitarian sort of device, the *jiaoyi* was a prestigious seat, offered to distinguished visitors as a matter of courtesy. Folding chairs were also used as ceremonial seats and thrones. Surviving folding chairs are beautifully carved and ornamented; a set in the Forbidden Palace is finished in black-and-gold lacquer. While decoration might be more or less elaborate, the basic design did not change for several

---

*The traditional Chinese character *jiao*, which means cross or exchange, includes a pictogram with crossed legs that resembles the X-frame of a folding chair.

Jiaoyi, *Chinese
folding chair*

hundred years. A seventeenth-century offshoot had a steeply re-clined back, a headrest, and long protruding arms. Since upper-class Chinese tended to sit upright, such slouching was considered inelegant, which may be why this chair was called *zui weng yi*, the "drunken old gentleman's chair."

It is likely the Chinese *zui weng yi* that was the model for a series of later European folding chairs. The British steamer chair, which originated in the late nine-teenth century, supported a similar semireclined posture. The steamer chair was all wood; the less expensive "deck chair" had a canvas sling seat. Such chairs were common at seaside resorts but, as the names suggest, probably origi-nated as outdoor chairs on ocean liners.* The *Titanic* car-ried six hundred steamer chairs, made of beechwood with slatted backs, woven rattan seats, and a hinged footrest that extended and turned the armchair into a chaise longue. This was the model for Kaare Klint's elegant oak-and-cane steamer chair, which improved the design by having the footrest slide out of the way when not in use. Klint also added a padded headrest.

My own deck chairs are of the simple wood-and-canvas variety that you still see in London parks. These chairs are tall enough to provide support for the head, and the backs can be adjusted to be more or less reclined; they come with

---

*The French called the deck chair *transat*, a shortening of *chaise transatlan-tique*.

and without arms. Although the deck chair is not a perfect chair—there is no lumbar support, and if I sit in it a long time the front rail cuts into my thighs—it is light and portable, and makes up for its limitations in convenience, folding perfectly flat when not in use. It is also inexpensive. The frugal Ludwig Wittgenstein furnished his rooms in Trinity College, Cambridge, with a pair of deck chairs. Were they gaily striped? I don't know, but I like to think that they evoked happy memories for the severe philosopher—as mine do for me: summer holidays at the beach, reading on the lawn, drinks at sundown.

The deck chair was associated with increased leisure time. Activities such as hunting, fishing, and hiking required folding furniture of a different sort—so-called camp furniture. In 1877, a British inventor, Joseph Beverley Fenby, received a patent for an unusual camp chair. The clever design consisted of interconnected X-frames onto which a canvas sling could be hung. The Fenby Chair (also called the Paragon Chair) did not require assembly but was simply unfolded; it was transported in a compact carry bag. The Harrods catalogue described the Fenby as "the most Portable Chair in the Market."

In the United States, the Fenby Chair was sold by Abercrombie & Fitch; Theodore Roosevelt was photographed in a Fenby while on safari in Africa. The chair was also used by the British and American military. The Italian version, manufactured in Tripoli and called the Tripolina, was the inspiration for a noncollapsible chair designed in 1938 by three Argentinian archi-

Fenby Chair
(Joseph Fenby)

tects. They replaced the wooden sticks with a rigid metal frame and changed the proportions to make the upright chair more like an easy chair. With its exaggerated sculptural look, the "butterfly chair" became a modernist favorite. When we were first married, we had two butterfly chairs in our sparsely furnished living room. We salvaged the frames from the back-lane trash and painted them, and my wife laboriously sewed the canvas slings. The chairs were comfortable once you dropped into them, although getting up could be awkward.

We also owned several director's chairs, which were used in the dining room. The director's chair, like the butterfly chair, assumed an iconic status among architects of my generation. If you couldn't afford a Cesca—and we couldn't—a director's chair was an acceptable substitute. Like the Fenby, it was a nineteenth-century invention, introduced in 1892 by the Gold Medal Camp Furniture Manufacturing Company of Racine, Wisconsin, which produced military, camping, and porch furniture. The wood-and-canvas folding armchair, patterned on the folding camp stool, may have been designed by Louis Latour, who was responsible for the company's bestselling folding cot. The collapsible armchair was intended for campers and yachtsmen, but in the early 1920s it gained an unintended clientele—and its name—thanks to the emerging Hollywood film industry. Directors and actors were often photographed on movie sets sitting on the lightweight, portable chairs. A hundred years later, these inexpensive chairs remain as popular as ever, and are still made by the Gold Medal Company, now located in Tennessee.

The most common outdoor folding chair today is the folding aluminum lawn chair, which comes as both an armchair and a chaise longue, the latter a worthy successor to

the deck chair. Invented in 1947 by
Fredric Arnold, a Brooklyn manufacturer, the chair is made of aluminum tubes and, unlike a director's
chair, follows the configuration of
a Chinese folding chair, although it
has none of its fluidity; indeed, the
lawn chair is downright homely.
You won't find an aluminum lawn
chair in a design museum, but perhaps you should. The chair does its
job extremely well: it is light (less
than four pounds); folded, it takes little space; it has arms;
and it can be left outside without rusting. Arnold's original
chair used canvas, but this was later replaced by nylon webbing.
This chair has none of the upper-class cachet and glamour of
the steamer chair or the safari chair; it is cheerfully plebeian—
which may be the reason that museums ignore it. Lawn chairs
are at home everywhere: on the beach, at tailgate parties and
suburban barbecues, or lining sidewalks for a Fourth of July
parade.

*Folding aluminum lawn
chair (Fredric Arnold)*

The lawn chair's indoor cousin is the ubiquitous metal
folding chair, a common presence at community events, church
suppers, bingo nights, and high school convocations—indeed,
anywhere temporary seating is required. The design of a
typical folding chair resembles a Chinese folding chair:
a two-piece X-frame of tubular metal, with a backrest and
a flip-down seat made of metal or plastic. This Plain Jane
chair is not terribly comfortable but it is adequate for an
hour or two; some versions are padded. Although high-end
furniture companies have produced fancy folding chairs,
this seems like gilding the lily or, perhaps, gilding the
dandelion.

Knockdown

The French and Italian words for furniture—*meubles* and *mobilia*—mean "movables" and date from the Middle Ages, when furniture accompanied its aristocratic owners as they moved from city house to country estate on their seasonal peregrinations. Benches and backstools were simply transported whole, but in order to be moved, tables and beds were taken apart—knocked down. In time, furniture became stationary, with occasional exceptions such as George Washington's trestle dining table. Demountable furniture came into its own in the late eighteenth century during the Napoleonic Wars. British officers stationed abroad expected to enjoy the comforts of home, and London outfitters provided a variety of travel items: trunks, spirits cases, and lap desks, as well as knockdown furniture in the form of bookshelves, beds, tables, and, of course, chairs. Most campaign chairs were simply conventional ones that could be disassembled by unscrewing the front legs and unbolting the seat from the back, although some dispensed with screws and bolts by hinging the various parts and using a drop-in seat to brace the frame. Early knockdown chairs were upholstered, but woven cane became increasingly popular because of its lightness. The Douro Chair, named after the Douro River in Portugal, where the British campaigned during the Peninsular War, was a caned easy chair with leather strap arms and loose horsehair cushions. The folded and disassembled parts fitted snugly inside a wooden box that, with the addition of screw-on legs, itself did double duty as a table. A "chair bed" was an armchair that folded out to resemble a chaise longue, and was particularly popular with ship's captains. Admiral Lord Nelson had a portable washstand and a writing box in his cabin on the *Victory*, although his favorite

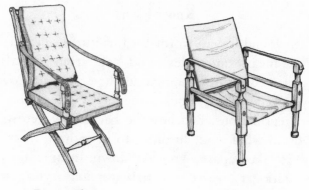

Douro Chair   *Roorkhee Chair*

armchair, a black-leather-upholstered easy chair with tufted cushions, was not collapsible. Campaign furniture was not only for the high and mighty. The London supplier J. W. Allen, who specialized in military equipage, offered a "barrack outfit" for junior officers: a collapsible iron bedstead, a chest, a washstand, and a Douro Chair, all for twenty-five pounds.

By the end of the nineteenth century, luxurious campaign furniture had been replaced by what we would call camp furniture. The Roorkhee Chair, named after the regimental headquarters of the Indian Army Corps of Engineers, was a mass-produced wood-and-canvas easy chair. The ten pieces of turned oak or mahogany, pegged in predrilled holes, were held together by two wing nuts and the laced canvas seat. Disassembled, the dowels and the canvas could be rolled into a compact bundle. The chair was not only quickly assembled and disassembled without tools, the frame was flexible enough to be stable no matter how uneven the ground.

The utilitarian Roorkhee Chair was used in Africa during the Boer War and later became popular with big-game hunters on safari. Its unknown inventor was likely a mem-

ber of the Corps of Engineers—the ingenious design has an
engineer's sense of straightforward functionality. No wonder
the chair influenced the early European modernists. Its leather-
strap arms showed up in Breuer's Wassily Chair, as well as
in Charlotte Perriand, Pierre Jeanneret, and Le Corbusier's
fauteuil à dossier basculant, a tubular steel armchair that
also copied the Roorkhee Chair's most comfortable feature,
a pivoting back. In 1933, after seeing a photograph of the
Roorkhee Chair, Kaare Klint modified the proportions,
simplified the turnings, made the seat lower and slightly
slanted, and produced his enduring Safari Chair. It includes
a modification suggested by Klint's friend Arne Jacobsen: a
loose seat cushion. The first Safari Chair I saw was in the
office of one of my professors, who had studied in Copenhagen. Soon after I graduated, I purchased one of my own, although all I could afford was a less-expensive imitation—a
copy of a copy.

Knockdown furniture was convenient for peripatetic
military officers, but in an age of international trade it had
another advantage: a demountable chair was cheaper to ship.
Many of Thonet's chairs, both bentwood and tubular steel,
were transported flat from the factory to his shops, where
they were assembled before delivery to customers. In 1925,
Theophilus Billington, who had owned a furniture store in
Dallas, received a patent for "a simple and inexpensive
table which may be manufactured and compactly shipped in
knocked-down condition but quickly and easily set up by the
merchant or other party receiving the shipment." A couple
of decades later, an Ohio furniture manufacturer, Erie J.
Sauder, began making ready-to-assemble furniture for a mail-
order company. But the major breakthrough in knockdown
furniture occurred elsewhere. In 1951, a Swedish draftsman,
Gillis Lundgren, had a eureka moment. He had bought a

table, and being unable to fit it into his Volvo, he unscrewed the legs and reassembled them when he got home. Lundgren worked for a mail-order company that sold furniture. Why not design furniture that could be shipped flat and was assembled by the buyer, he reasoned. He mentioned his idea to his employer, Ingvar Kamprad, and a few years later the company produced its first piece of knockdown furniture. Needless to say, I am describing IKEA.

Anyone who has struggled to assemble an IKEA product will have mixed feelings about Lundgren's discovery. Over the years I have put together a table and several IKEA bookshelves and cupboards, but never a chair. As a test, I bought the most basic wooden chair in the IKEA catalogue, a side chair called Ivar.* The chair cost twenty-five dollars and came in a flat cardboard box only four inches thick. IKEA's wooden furniture is made in one of forty-four plants located in eleven countries; my chair came from China. There were seven pieces: two side frames, two slats, two rails, and a seat, all unpainted wood. There was also a plastic bag of assorted hardware and an Allen wrench. I counted the ten screws and sixteen wooden pegs before starting because I remembered that IKEA doesn't provide extras. I carefully read the instruction booklet, which resembled a comic strip without words. There were six steps, and it seemed clear enough except for step five, which included "Do" and "Don't" diagrams that to me looked identical. Undeterred, I plunged ahead.

"IKEA is Legos for grownups, connecting the furniture of our adulthoods with the toys of our childhoods," wrote Lauren Collins in *The New Yorker*. I'm not convinced by

---

*All IKEA products are given names. Chairs have men's names, outdoor furniture is named after Swedish islands, dining sets are named after Finnish islands, and so on.

Ivar (IKEA)

the analogy because I've never actually enjoyed assembling IKEA products, but it took only fifteen minutes to put Ivar together, which included going down to the basement when I realized that I needed a Phillips screwdriver. The result was a simple ladder-back chair with a flat wooden seat. It was not without small refinements: the back was slightly inclined, the slats were gently curved, the seat was subtly wedge-shaped, and the rear legs were splayed, giving the chair an attractive stance.

I field-tested Ivar for a week as a dining chair. It was more comfortable than I expected, despite the flat seat. Or perhaps because of it? Galen Cranz, a Berkeley architecture professor who has written about the ergonomics of chairs, is a proponent of flat, uncontoured seats that allow more body movement than shaped seats. Sitting in the chair, I could feel the lower slat giving lumbar support and my upper back resting against the top rail. Not quite an Åkerblom curve, but close.

My wife kept asking me how long the IKEA chair was going to stay in the dining room. I had to admit that compared with our bentwood chairs Ivar was a clumsy fellow. You couldn't really blame him—he was made of white pine. Plentiful and easily worked softwoods such as pine were traditionally used only by country carpenters; joiners and cabinetmakers used hardwoods. Comparing white pine with beech (which is what our bentwood chairs are made of), it is easy to understand why. The compressive and bending strengths of beech are twice that of pine; beech is also four times harder. This means that a beechwood chair can be more delicate than a pine chair—hence lighter—and it will be more resistant to wear and tear. Beech is also more stable than pine, less likely to warp, and more amenable to carving. Finally, the surface of oiled or varnished hardwoods is visually richer. The reason that IKEA uses pine in its least expensive chairs is simply price; pine is two to three times cheaper than beech. On the other hand, a softwood chair's life expectancy is considerably shorter than that of a good hardwood chair, which can last for centuries. Poor old Ivar is unlikely to ever see the inside of a consignment shop.

Swing

Folding and knockdown chairs can be easily transported, but what about chairs that move in place? The first moving seats were not rockers, which we have already examined, but swings. The oldest representation of one that I came across was a clay figurine of a girl sitting on a swing suspended between two posts or trees. It was discovered in Hagia Triada, a late Minoan settlement dating from the middle of the second millennium B.C. Whether the figurine is a cult object or a toy is unclear, but the bench seat is immediately recognizable, as is the figure's familiar posture, two raised arms grasping the ropes.

There is something pleasantly aimless about sitting on a swing, although it does require concentration—you can't read, or eat, or doze off. Swinging is the closest thing to flying, the rush of air, the rhythmic movement, the ever-ascending arc. Swings, because they are so simple—a board and two ropes—appeared independently in many different cultures. Greek amphora paintings depict women on improvised swings—four-legged stools suspended from tree branches by ropes—a reference to the Dionysian Feast of the Swing. Pre-Columbian figurines depict children on swings, which is hardly surprising since the hammock was a Mayan invention. Old Chinese paintings show women standing on garden swings, and swing competitions were a feature of traditional village festivals in China and Korea. In Japan, the garden swing was probably a European import, for it was called *buranko*, the Japanese pronunciation of the Portuguese *balanco*.

Swings are popular on the Indian subcontinent, where they were introduced by the Mughals. Miniature Rajput paintings show women seated and standing on garden swings, singly and in pairs. Today, Indian swings, or *jhoolas*, come in a variety of sizes, as small as an infant's cradle or as large as a king-size bed, and are used inside homes as well as in gardens. According to a Gujarati friend, a key pleasure of a *jhoola* is the cooling breeze as it swings.

Indian swings, like the swings of antiquity, are associated with women. In a contemporary Indian novel, *Beyond Diamond Rings* by Kusum Choppra, one of the female characters wonders about this. "Isn't it curious that except for the trapeze artists, you never see men on swings? It is always women and girls who are on the swings, in the gardens, the public parks, the playgrounds, the private jhoolas at homes, everywhere, all the time, in art, in literature, in songs, in festivals, in the seasons, whatever." She later concludes that it is the sense of freedom experienced on a swing that attracts women. "Up there, you are one with the clouds, the birds, and the air. Those velvet lined, gold chains around the ankles are left behind down there, somewhere, as you soar high on your imagination . . ."

There is something mildly erotic about a young woman lightheartedly swinging to and fro, hair and dress aswirl. Rococo painters certainly thought so, and young women on swings were a staple of artists such as Watteau. Eighteenth-century swings were not pushed but pulled—by a rope attached to the swing, usually handled by a young man. The back-and-forth movement of the swing—now tantalizingly close, now untouchably far—was a fitting painterly metaphor for the ritual of courtship. The great swing masterpiece was painted by François Boucher's pupil Jean-Honoré Fragonard. Originally titled *The Happy Accidents of the Swing*, the painting portrays a pretty young woman on a swing in a garden. Her elderly guardian—or perhaps spouse—is sitting on a bench behind her, pulling on the rope. Unknown to him, a handsome young admirer is hidden in the rosebushes. As the woman reaches the high point of her swing, she kicks up her leg with gay abandon, sending one pink shoe flying in the voyeur's direction, while he gazes rapturously up her billowing skirts.

Pierre-Auguste Renoir, who admired Fragonard, painted a woman on a swing, too. His version is almost the opposite of Fragonard's suggestive scene. The setting is a public garden in Montmartre, suffused in dappled light. A young woman is standing motionless on a low swing, engaged in intimate conversation with a man who may be courting her; perhaps he has just proposed. If so, he is not doing well, for she has turned away, seemingly embarrassed. In French, a swing is a *balançoire*, and her somewhat precarious posture appears distinctly *un*balanced, mirroring her indecision.

Had Renoir been American rather than French, and had he lived in a small town rather than a city, he might have set his painting on a porch and placed his model on a swing seat. Porch swings were—and are—an American fixture. They probably originated in the South, where the climate encouraged their use and "porch life" was a long-standing tradition. Like the *jhoola*, the southern swing was often

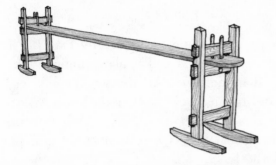

*Lowcountry
joggling board*

couch-size. Like rococo swings, porch swings were associated with romance, specifically courtship. Swings were not
used inside the house, but were sometimes used as beds on
sleeping porches. Starting at the turn of the nineteenth
century, New England sailmakers made swing beds called
"couch hammocks," which were deep, box-shaped settees
made out of scrap canvas laced with rope. They were likewise used outside on porches, the high back and sides providing protection from the wind.

Charleston, South Carolina, is a city closely associated
with swings, because so many houses have verandas. That
is where I first saw an unusual porch seat: the so-called
joggling board. The seat resembles a very long bench—
sometimes as long as sixteen feet—with a flexible plank,
usually southern yellow pine, freely supported at each end,
which allows the sitter to bounce up and down. Sometimes
the supports are on rockers. The joggling board is supposed to have originated in the early 1800s on a Lowcountry
plantation whose owner's sister suffered from rheumatism;
the springy bench enabled her to exercise in place. I was told
that in the past, courting couples would sit at opposite ends
of the board, and as the bench bounced, they would slide
closer together until they met in the middle. Think of what
Fragonard could have done with that.

Roll

The other evening my wife and I saw *As You Like It* performed by a local theater company. The play contains Shakespeare's oft-quoted monologue "All the world's a stage." The Seven Ages of Man made me think of the Seven Ages of Chairs: baby carriage, high chair, schoolroom chair, office chair, club chair, recliner, wheelchair. Our lives begin and end in chairs on wheels.

I have a photograph of myself in a stroller on Crossland Crescent in Peebles, Scotland, in 1945. I am two years old, slouched, asleep. The stroller is rudimentary: four wheels attached to a tubular steel frame with a seat and a push bar. The seat must be metal or some other hard material, for it is covered with a blanket. This type of baby carriage was descended from the perambulator, or pram, a late-nineteenth-century Victorian invention that was essentially a bassinet on wheels. Prams were large, elaborate, and expensive—I doubt that my parents could have afforded one on a second lieutenant's pay. A stroller, or pushchair, as the British called it, was a much cheaper alternative.

Owen Finlay Maclaren, a British aeronautical engineer, is the Thomas Edison of the stroller. During World War II, he was responsible for the design of the retractable undercarriage of the Spitfire fighter plane. After the war, Maclaren started a company that made aluminum aircraft parts, and also explored using the new lightweight material for consumer products. In 1961, he produced the Gadabout, a folding camp chair that is an updated—and simplified—descendant of the Fenby Chair. Four tubular aluminum X-frames support a fabric sling. This chair was the immediate precursor to his classic umbrella stroller. Maclaren had the idea when he saw his daughter, who was visiting from the

Umbrella stroller
(Owen Maclaren)

United States with his first grand-child, struggling with a conventional baby carriage. He designed a collapsible pushchair that is basically the Gadabout on wheels. The tubular aluminum X-frames support a polyethylene fabric sling seat, and the whole thing, which weighs only six pounds, handily folds up into a compact bundle—like an umbrella. (Using a foot release lever, a person holding a baby can fold and unfold the stroller with one hand.)

Maclaren's chair is in the collection of the Museum of Modern Art, but unlike most designer chairs it is not an aesthetic object but a tool, as functional as a fighter-plane undercarriage.

Maclaren's stroller reminds me of an earlier child's chair. In 1760, Louis XV charged the great *ébéniste* Jean-François Oeben with an unusual commission: a special wheelchair. It was for the king's oldest grandson, the nine-year-old Duke of Burgundy, Louis-Joseph, who was unable to walk as the result of a recent accident—he fell off a hobby horse. Only this written description survives of Oeben's creation:

> Delivered by le Seigneur Oeben, cabinetmaker, for the use of M. le Duc de Bourgoyne at Versailles, a mechanical armchair with springs, 30 in. wide and 30 in. high, rotating on a pivot and rising to a height of 5½ ft., covered with crimson damask with cushions in two sections and a third for the back, all in crimson, the head rest in the same color of damask, there is a footrest covered in red-morocco leather under which is a frame of polished iron containing six brass wheels

which engage into a worm-screw, at the foot are three brass castors for rolling the chair and turning it in any direction. Note: Three wheels, two large and one small, have been attached to the chair to enable it to be taken out into the park, and a kind of swan-neck supporting a wooden canopy to which to attach curtains, and there is a table in cherry-wood.

The little duke, who died before his tenth birthday, did not get much use from this magical contraption.

It is difficult to imagine a rotating chair that is also capable of rising to a height of five feet, but the reference to a "worm-screw" makes Oeben's mechanical chair sound like the invalid's chair invented a hundred years earlier by Nicolas Grollier de Servière, a military engineer. Grollier had a "cabinet of curiosities" in his Lyon residence where he displayed working models of his inventions—siege engines, hydraulic machines, surveying instruments, locks, clocks, and windmills. The count was the Leonardo of his day—so famous that no lesser than Louis XIV traveled to Lyon to see the collection. Among the displays was a self-propelled chair with two geared front wheels powered by worm gears turned by hand cranks. By operating one or both of the cranks, the sitter could move the chair backward or forward, this way or that. The mechanical chair was included in a catalogue of Grollier's works published by his grandson in 1719: "very useful for the lame and for those with gout, which can be used to move around a home on one level or in the garden, without anyone's help." Parisian joiners were soon building self-propelled *fauteuils de malade*, with padded armrests, loose seat cushions, and reclining backrests. Oeben, with his interest in mechanical devices, would undoubtedly have been familiar with such chairs.

Fauteuil de malade,
eighteenth century

Grollier's mechanical chair was introduced to England by John Joseph Merlin, a Belgian-born mathematical-instrument maker and inventor. Merlin opened a private museum in London where he exhibited his inventions: lifelike automatons, ingenious music boxes, complicated timepieces, weigh scales, and mechanical toys. His self-propelled "Gouty Chair" was a direct copy of a *fauteuil de malade*, but Merlin subsequently made an original contribution to the evolution of the wheelchair. He substituted two large push wheels for the hand-cranked front wheels, producing an invalid's chair that could be used out of doors. In addition, he is credited with adding external hoops to the push wheels so that sitters could avoid handling the dirty tires. Often fitted with reclining backs and footrests, "Merlin chairs" were widely used in Britain throughout the nineteenth century and were the forerunners of today's wheelchairs.

The modern collapsible wheelchair was the work of a pair of British mechanical engineers, Herbert Everest and Harry Jennings. Everest had broken his back in a mining accident, and he needed a wheelchair that could be folded and put in the trunk of a car. In 1933, he and his friend Jennings built a chair that used lightweight tubular steel, a canvas seat and back, and an X-frame that allowed the chair to fold flat like a director's chair. Everest and Jennings formed a company, and their collapsible design became the international standard.

If you go into any hospital today you will find folding wheelchairs that are essentially unchanged since the Everest

and Jennings design of eighty years
ago. In 2009, Michael Graves, himself a wheelchair user ever since
being paralyzed by an infection,
was asked by Stryker, a manufacturer of medical equipment, to
take a second look at the hospital
transport wheelchair. Graves and
his team identified several problems with conventional wheelchairs: they were designed to be
self-propelled, although hospital

Transport wheel chair
(Michael Graves)

chairs were pushed by attendants who frequently suffered
back strain because of the awkward placement of the bicycle-
type handles; attendants were obliged to bend down each
time they adjusted the footrests; and the large wheels were a
liability, as they not only tended to bump into things, they
picked up infections from the floor and transmitted them to
the patient. Not least, hospitals were constantly restocking
wheelchairs because the collapsible model was highly susceptible to theft.

The Graves solution looks very different from the familiar
Everest and Jennings design. The chair does not fold, although
it nests to save space. The rear wheels are about a foot in
diameter, and out of reach of the patient. Arm- and footrests
swing out of the way, and the brake and footrest controls do
not require the attendant to bend down but are foot acti-
vated. The vertical push handles comfortably accommodate
attendants of different heights. Because the wheelchair is
not collapsible, the seat and backrest are cushiony molded
plastic rather than fabric slings—much more comfortable.

The Graves wheelchair is a simple design. The front members extend from the small casters and footrests, support the

backrest, and become the push handles; the back members extend from the larger wheels to support the seat, and become the armrests. The shape of the armrests assists in getting up. The steel frame is white and the plastic parts are dark blue; the critical control points—footrest and armrest releases and the brake pedal—are highlighted in bright yellow.

Like the Everest and Jennings wheelchair, Graves's transport chair is a tool that addresses utilitarian problems—and looks it. Graves was a high-fashion architect, not an engineer, but although he designed a famously whimsical whistling tea kettle, his transport chair conforms to the convention that hospital equipment should be "serious"—no frills. Not that a mobile chair *has* to appear mechanical. We don't know what Oeben's *fauteuil méchanique* looked like, but a surviving eighteenth-century *fauteuil de malade* is a handsome beechwood armchair upholstered in dark red leather—a domestic easy chair that just happens to be on wheels. Voltaire's invalid's chair has survived too, a green velvet armchair on casters that speaks of the salon, not the sickroom. Both are reminders that form does not follow function, it follows culture. Perhaps one day hospital furnishings will look homey rather than institutional—that might not be a bad thing.

ELEVEN

Human Engineering

Chairs existed in dynastic China, Georgian England, Colonial America, and fin-de-siècle Vienna. The methods of manufacture varied, from sophisticated to crude, from handcrafted to industrialized, yet the yokeback chair, the cabriole, the sack-back, and the bentwood chair share essential qualities. They demonstrate that a chair, however it is made, is always a chair; it has legs, a back, a seat, and frequently arms. Chairs have accommodated different postures—more or less upright, more or less relaxed—but the human body is a constant. Or is it?

To begin with, the average male is taller than the average female, with wider shoulders and narrower hips. These differences are compounded because men and women come in distinct body types—endomorph (rotund), mesomorph (muscular and bony), and ectomorph (thin and delicate)—and many combinations in between. Although it is possible to establish statistical means, there is no such thing as an "average adult." People of average weight are not necessarily of average height, those of average height vary in weight, those of average arm span have different-length torsos, and so on. And there are racial differences: East Asians tend to have shorter legs and arms than Caucasians; Africans, longer.

How can the same chair comfortably accommodate a five-foot, hundred-pound female and a six-foot, two-hundred-pound male? The right armrest height for one person is wrong for another; a chair deep enough for a six-footer will be awkward for a shorter person, and vice versa. One traditional solution was to provide different sizes of chairs. Seventeenth-century Flemish family portraits typically show the father occupying a large armchair, the mother in a smaller armchair, a slightly smaller side chair for the grandmother, and miniature chairs for the children. French eighteenth-century chairs such as the bergère and the *chauffeuse*, which were intended for women, had smaller dimensions than a typical fauteuil, although they were often wider to accommodate women's full skirts. Then a subtle shift occurred: cabinet-makers began to make chairs that could be adjusted to suit the sitter. The first modification was an adjustable reclining back, which appeared first in wing chairs and in *fauteuils de malade*. Adjustable reclining chairs in the form of steamer chairs and deck chairs became popular in the second half of the nineteenth century. These were outdoor chairs, but an indoor reclining chair appeared during the same period. The Morris chair, designed by the Arts and Crafts architect Philip Webb and named after his friend William Morris, was a low wooden armchair with a hinged back whose angle could be altered by degrees. The design migrated to the United States where, adapted by Gustav Stickley, it became a staple of the Craftsman style.

Adjustable chairs were driven by a desire for comfort, but in some settings functionality was the main concern. Dentists, for example, required adjustable chairs. The first American dental chair is credited to Josiah Flagg, Jr., a Boston dentist who in the 1790s added an adjustable padded headrest to a continuous-arm Windsor chair. Reclining backs followed. Barbers, too, needed adjustability; customers had to be upright for haircutting but prone for shaving. In 1904, Samuel Kline of Trenton, New Jersey, filed a patent for a barber chair that incorporated "adjustable seat and back members . . . with a combined foot and leg rest which latter is so constructed as to be readily adjusted to and from the chair to accommodate persons of different heights." About the same time as Kline was patenting his barber chair, Josef Hoffmann was designing a chair for sanatorium patients: the *Sitzmaschine* with a reclining back and a pull-out footrest.

Medical chairs led the way in adjustability. In 1922, Jean Pascaud, a Parisian physician, introduced an anatomical chaise longue that he called *Le Sur-repos*, which means something like "the restful chair." Intended for convalescents, the light and elegant chair had a padded seat on a tubular steel base, with a steeply reclining back and a movable headrest. The hinged armrests swung out of the way to facilitate sitting down or getting up. Turning a large wheel on the side rotated the angle of the chair, raising the legs and lowering the head.

In 1928, inspired by Dr. Pascaud, Le Corbusier, Charlotte Perriand, and Pierre Jeanneret designed a tubular steel contoured chaise longue that sat in a cradle so the overall angle could similarly be altered. The Thonet B306 was widely admired by architects but was not a commercial success, perhaps because it lacked arms, which made it uncomfortable. You also had to get out of the chair to change the angle. A British offshoot of the *Sur-repos* was Foot's Adjustable Rest-Chair, a domestic easy chair, likewise with hinged arms. This lounge chair could be converted into a chaise longue thanks to a padded footrest that was concealed under the seat. "Simply press a button and the back declines or automatically rises," reads the advertisement. "Release the button and the back is instantly locked." The Rest-Chair resembled a wing chair, and with its paisley-patterned upholstery it looked resolutely old-fashioned, although it was arguably a more advanced "resting machine" than Le Corbusier's clumsy contraption.

Starting in 1937, Gebrüder Thonet produced an unusual convalescent chair. The designers were the architect brothers Hans and Wassili Luckhardt. The Luckhardts were leading Berlin modernists, but their chair was not a typical Bauhaus product. For one thing, it was made out of wood. With contoured slats and an extendable footrest, it recalled a steamer chair. The resemblance was skin-deep, however, for this was a true mechanical chair. The Luckhardts called it a "movement chair" because the back, seat, and footrest were interconnected, so that as the sitter shifted position, the three parts moved together; tightening a knob fixed the desired angle. Thonet marketed the chair as "Siesta-Medizinal," and during World War II adapted it for hospitals, using a tubular steel frame with coiled springs supporting a full-length leather pad. A wheelchair version accommodated injured servicemen. Aldous Huxley's "hospital style of furnishing" had finally come home.

The Luckhardt brothers also designed chairs for Thonet's Berlin-based competitor, Deutsche Stahlmöbel (German Steel Furniture), known as DESTA. The owner of DESTA was Anton Lorenz, a significant if somewhat shadowy presence on the Berlin prewar avant-garde furniture scene. Lorenz was neither an architect nor a craftsman; he is sometimes described as a businessman, but he wasn't exactly that either. In some ways he resembles his contempo-

Siesta-Medizinal reclining chair
(Hans and Wassili Luckhardt)

rary Buckminster Fuller—an inventor-entrepreneur. Born in Budapest, Lorenz accompanied his wife, Irene, an opera singer, to Leipzig. In time, he acquired a metalworking business that made locks. In Berlin, Lorenz met his compatriot Kalman Lengyel and became a partner in Standard Möbel, fabricating Marcel Breuer's tubular furniture in his workshop. After the company was taken over by Thonet, Lorenz continued in the chair business on his own. He demonstrated an unexpected flair for design, as well as proving to be a canny businessman. He had earlier independently registered his own version of a cantilever chair (something that Breuer had neglected to do with the Cesca), and in addition he also acquired the rights to Mart Stam's cantilever chair. With this legal ammunition, Lorenz sued Thonet, the largest furniture company in the world, for infringement of copyright—and won.

Lorenz ultimately reached an agreement with Thonet. His company, DESTA, continued to produce tubular steel furniture designed by himself, the Luckhardts, and prominent architects such as Erich Mendelsohn and Otto Rittweger (Mies van der Rohe and Le Corbusier resisted Lorenz's overtures). Lorenz, who was interested in human physiology, engaged the Kaiser Wilhelm Institute to carry out experiments in body posture, photographing subjects in a saltwater tank to document body positions in a situation of near weightlessness. In 1939, he and Hans Luckhardt filed a joint U.S. patent for an adjustable reclining chair with a pivoting footrest that rose as the back of the chair reclined. As we shall see, this device would have a key role in the development of a new kind of chair.

When Germany invaded Poland, Lorenz and his wife were in California on business, and they decided to stay in the United States, where Lorenz continued to work on chairs. He met Mies van der Rohe in Chicago, and the two patented a conchoidal plastic chair, never produced. Lorenz formed a more productive association with Edward J. Barcalo of Buffalo, whose company made a range of metal furniture—hospital beds, cribs, and garden furniture. Barcalo licensed Lorenz and Luckhardt's reclining mechanism, and in 1946 produced a tubular steel reclining lawn chair, marketed as the BarcaLoafer, as well as a version of the Siesta wheelchair for returning veterans.

Lorenz and Barcalo's ultimate goal was to produce a reclining chair for the home. This required a different design, because while Americans liked inexpensive chromed-steel dining sets and metal lawn chairs, most people did not consider tubular steel furniture appropriate for the living room. In 1947, the Barcalo Company merged with Chandler Industries, a Buffalo furniture manufacturer, in order to produce a fully upholstered reclining chair. Barcalo provided the mechanism based on Lorenz's design; Chandler manufactured the body of the chair. The BarcaLounger was born.

The stately BarcaLounger was entirely unlike its Bauhaus ancestor. The reclining machinery was concealed within a plushy carapace of wood framing and sprung upholstery, resulting in a conservatively styled armchair that sacrificed lightness for comfort. Closed, the chair looked like an ordinary upholstered easy chair, but when the sitter pulled a lever the back reclined and a padded footrest swung up. The so-called recliner was first marketed to white-collar execu-

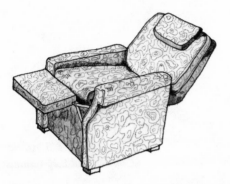

1950s BarcaLounger

tives; a 1955 magazine advertisement shows a man in a business suit sitting in what is described as "the chair that's teaching America how to relax." That was not hyperbole; as prices fell, the recliner attracted a wide audience—mostly male—and became the iconic lounge chair of Middle America.* Recliners were designed to appeal to the widest possible range of tastes; they came in the form of club chairs, wing chairs, and easy chairs, made by companies with catchy names such as Rock-A-Fella, Stratolounger, Slumber Chair, and, of course, La-Z-Boy, another pioneer in the field. Lorenz, with his many patents, benefitted financially from this popularity. One of his last inventions—he died in 1964—was a recliner that provided an intermediate position between upright and horizontal: the television-watching chair.

In 1956, in a direct response to the American recliner craze, the Herman Miller company produced a lounge chair designed by Charles and Ray Eames. It was made out of three molded plywood shells—seat, back, and headrest—attached to a metal base with rubber shock mounts. The interior of the shell was heavily padded with foam and upholstered in

---

*Archie Bunker, the character in the popular television series *All in the Family*, did not sit in a recliner, but in a worn wing chair.

*Lounge chair and ottoman
(Charles and Ray Eames)*

leather. The veneered shells were Brazilian rosewood and the soft black leather was tufted, giving the chair a luxurious appearance. Although not adjustable, the swiveling chair came with an ottoman and provided the same plushy, legs-up experience as a recliner. Ray Eames described it as "comfortable and un-designy."

The Eames chair was intended for the high-end market, and Herman Miller was careful to call it a "lounge chair," not to be confused with the plebeian recliner. Urban sophisticates scorned the recliner as a symbol of slothfulness and indolence, and derided its conservative styling. President Kennedy's folksy rocking chair was chic; President Johnson's turquoise leather recliner was not. Of course, this was mainly snobbery. Like fins on cars, Dagwood sandwiches, and leisure suits, the American recliner was simply déclassé.

Problem-solving

In the late 1970s, Herman Miller, now a leader in high-design residential and office furniture, took aim at the fastest-growing population segment in the country—the elderly—

and commissioned the designers William Stumpf and Don Chadwick to design a chair. The pair decided to focus on the recliner because it was popular with older people and was used not only in homes but also in retirement communities, assisted-living facilities, and even hospitals. They concluded that existing recliners were ill-suited to extended use because the cushiony seats did not offer good support, and the non-breathable upholstery material, typically leather or Nauga-hyde, could actually cause bedsores. They substituted a breathable plastic mesh that was cooler and offered better support. They called their product the Sarah Chair.

It took a decade to develop the Sarah Chair, but by then Herman Miller had gotten cold feet. One problem was mar-keting. Recliners were typically sold in mainstream furniture outlets and department stores, not the kinds of places that carried Herman Miller chairs. Moreover, the public associ-ated the recliner with mainstream taste, and the company feared that a Herman Miller recliner might actually hurt the high-design brand. The project was shelved.

Several years later, Herman Miller asked Stumpf and Chadwick to adapt some of the ideas from the Sarah Chair to a more conventional product: an office chair. The general configuration of office chairs was well established by this time. The secretarial chair was an armless swivel chair on casters, with adjustable height and back. Next in the office chair hierarchy was the managerial chair, with arms and a tilt-back mechanism. At the top of the pyramid was the ex-ecutive chair, usually leather and with a taller back. A typi-cal executive chair of the 1960s had a swivel-tilt mechanism and two controls: seat height and tilt tension—everything else was fixed.

Swivel-tilt chairs, which originated in the middle of the nineteenth century, were originally intended for the home—

they were, in effect, mechanical rocking chairs. They were usually low-back Windsor chairs or fully upholstered easy chairs. By the early 1900s, these had evolved into banker's chairs and stenographer's chairs, although it took several decades for the office chair to gain wide acceptance. A 1912 photograph of the *New York Times* newsroom shows the pressmen sitting not on office chairs but on Thonet N. 18 café chairs.

Stumpf had already designed an office chair for Herman Miller. Unlike other office chairs, his tilted in such a way that the feet stayed flat on the floor. In addition to the usual tilt-back controls, the user could also adjust the height and angle of the back, and the height, width, and angle of the arms. There was a further refinement. Studies had shown that in terms of body weight and height as much as 11 percent of the workforce fell outside the statistical norm, so the chair, called the Ergon, came in two sizes: small and large.

Stumpf and Chadwick incorporated the adjustable features of the Ergon Chair into their design, added lumbar support, and went one better by providing *three* sizes: small, medium, and large. They also did something more radical— they got rid of the upholstery. The Ergon Chair, like all office chairs, had a thick fabric-covered foam seat and back. Taking their cue from the Sarah Chair, the designers substituted woven plastic mesh, which resembled traditional caning but was more resilient.* Unlike the Sarah, which had thin padding, the mesh was left exposed. The absence of padding increased breathability, which reduced the buildup of body heat that normally occurs in a foam-padded chair. The paper-thin

---

*This was not the first application of plastic mesh in a chair. As early as 1966, Richard Schultz designed a line of outdoor furniture—side chair, lounge chair, chaise longue—using vinyl-coated polyester mesh stretched on cast and extruded aluminum frames.

Aeron Chair
(William Stumpf and
Don Chadwick)

and semitransparent mesh gave the chair its name—Aeron.

The Aeron Chair was a new type of office chair, not an executive chair, nor a managerial chair, nor an office chair, but a "task chair." It could be used interchangeably in executive offices, conference rooms, and workstations, and it suited a wide range of white-collar workers— executives, managers, financial traders, and software programmers. The Aeron was launched in 1994, the height of the dot-com boom, and the unconventional all-black chair, which represented a rejection of the traditional corporate chair hierarchy, became especially popular in the upstart Internet industry. The chair's relatively high price made it a status symbol, like a Rolex watch or a BMW car. Exactly what the Aeron chair will symbolize in the future is harder to guess; will it stand for the advent of ergonomic comfort in the office, the ascendancy of the sedentary white-collar workplace in the digital age, or simply the hubris of the dot-com bubble?

My first writing chair was a used banker's chair. According to the stenciled information under the seat, it was made in Kitchener, Ontario, in 1963. The rotating maple armchair on casters had a tilt mechanism that lifted my feet off the ground whenever I leaned back. Only the height was adjustable, and that required kneeling down to turn a disk that raised or lowered the threaded center post. The seat was carved with a saddle-shaped depression that was comfortable for short periods, although I eventually bought a seat cushion, the kind with two ribbons that are tied to the back slats. Never mind, whenever I sat in it I felt like Pat O'Brien in *The Front Page*.

I still have my banker's chair, but the chair I write in daily is an Aeron, which I bought shortly after it appeared. It's a perfectly fine chair. The controls work, and the mesh is pleasant to sit on, especially in the summer. If I have any reservations about it, they concern the chair's somewhat antiseptic character. The chair may be 94 percent recyclable as the manufacturer claims, but while the wooden armrests of my banker's chair are pleasantly worn where countless hands have rubbed them, I've written nine books in my Aeron, and its rubber armrests look exactly the same as the day I bought it.* Such mechanical perfection is slightly intimidating, rather than endearing.

The Chair Becomes a Scale

Following the success of the all-adjustable Aeron, virtually all office chairs sprouted knobs, buttons, and levers. There was a problem with so much adjustability, however, as a writer pointed out in *Slate*. "Most people are not the first to use their office chairs. By the time you get a third-hand chair, the settings have been messed with hundreds of times and the instruction booklet is long gone. Even if you manage to figure out what each lever does, you often feel unsure of yourself—with so many possible adjustment permutations, you always suspect that you've chosen a suboptimal mix." Niels Diffrient, an industrial designer, was even more critical. "It occurred to me that the chairs on the market at the

---

*Trumpeting recyclability is a major part of marketing office task chairs, which is odd given that a well-made chair will last for generations.

time called 'ergonomic' were fakes, most of them," he told an interviewer. "They were putting up a visual depiction of something that looked like it was technically adapted to human use. But when you looked into it, you found that it was a sham. It was a visual seduction. There were many of them, quite handsome. Nice chairs in many ways, but the claims of them being ergonomic fell short."

Diffrient was introduced to chair design early in his career. While studying at Cranbrook Academy in the late 1940s, he supported himself by working part-time as a model maker in the Saarinen & Saarinen office. One of his responsibilities was assisting Eero Saarinen in the design of an executive office chair. Diffrient described Saarinen's working method. "You got what you got by throwing away everything that wasn't as good—but you tried everything. I had thought it was going to be a simple job of doing a chair with him for a month or two, but it was a year's effort."

In 1955, the young Diffrient joined the office of Henry Dreyfuss. Dreyfuss, who is considered a founding father of American industrial design, was responsible for the design of such iconic everyday objects as the first tabletop telephone, the upright vacuum cleaner, and the circular wall thermostat. Dreyfuss was not a stylist; his success was based on analysis and close observation, combined with a systematic study of human measurements, which he called "human engineering." In 1960, he published a folio of loose information sheets that summarized his offices's research on the human body in graphic form. *The Measure of Man* was widely circulated among industrial designers and architects.

After Dreyfuss retired, Diffrient, now a partner, spearheaded a project that vastly expanded the information sheets into a three-volume reference work titled *Humanscale*. This veritable encyclopedia of body measurements included information on children, adolescents, the elderly, and the handicapped, as well as specifications on human strength and safety, the workplace, and space planning. The section on seating pointed out the importance of using ergonomic data: "Some chairs today look as though the designer never saw a human body—they do not conform to body curves, they overload certain tissues to the point of fatigue, and they do not support the hollow of the back. Most people are so accustomed to poor seating that they accept discomfort as a matter of course, and when purchasing a chair they often place more importance on its appearance than on its comfort." The last comment echoes Franz Staffel's observation of a century earlier, that most chairs were "constructed more for the eye than for the back."

Diffrient had worked on a variety of product designs—the Trimline phone, the SX-70 Polaroid Land camera, tractors for John Deere—but he was drawn to furniture. In 1981, at the age of fifty-three, he left the Dreyfuss office to strike out on his own. As he laconically wrote in his autobiography, "I decided to direct my future design activities toward commercial furniture, principally seating." One of the problems that consumed Diffrient was an office chair that could accommodate different-size people in different positions. Experience had taught him to distrust complicated controls. While with Dreyfuss, he had designed an airplane seat for American Airlines with a pneumatic lumbar support that passengers could adjust by pressing a button. "It was designed simply for two things—to adapt to a person's particular form and to make it possible for him to change the shape of the back once in a while, just for the sake of change," Diffrient explained. The airline provided instructions on how to use the control but few people bothered to read them. "The sad thing is that people generally don't perceive that this does them good and didn't bother to learn how to use the adjustment, so in time the airlines figured that it wasn't selling more tickets and abandoned it."

Continuing in the direction begun by the Luckhardt brothers and Anton Lorenz, Diffrient developed a prototype office chair with a counterbalanced tilting mechanism that automatically provided the right amount of support through the full range of reclining motions, regardless of body size and weight, without a need for the sitter to fiddle with controls. By this time, Diffrient had turned seventy and his tinkering with chairs—he didn't have a client for his counterbalanced chair—must have seemed like an expensive hobby, or even an obsession. Then, as he put it, fate intervened.

In January 1998 a very tall young man came through my door announcing that he was looking for someone to design a chair for the company he owned. His name was Bob King and he had been searching for a designer to design an ergonomic task chair to fit in with the rest of his product line. His company was, to my surprise, not a furniture company in the traditional sense; he focused on "ergonomic aids for the office" . . . His products were high quality and unique so his sales and growth had been impressive. Yet, he remained a relatively small company and felt an ergonomic chair would broaden his line and propel sales and status to a new level . . . I then rolled in the prototype of my ergonomic chair design and said, "Is this what you had in mind?" I proceeded to demonstrate the features and at each step I could see he was getting more excited. At the end of my comments he said, "When can we start? It's exactly what I want."

Diffrient assembled a team and got to work. He approached chair design as a set of interrelated problems. "When I design a chair I design it by sub-actions," he explained. "That is, the armrest is one action, the seat height's another action, the backrest tilt's another action. All those are separate actions. Each one has to be efficient and use the right material. I have always started with a process that allows me to work those things out on an isolated basis before I worry about how it's going to look." In other words, like his mentor Dreyfuss, Diffrient did not start with an inspirational sketch, a concept, or a predetermined form, but with an analysis of the problem from the user's point of view.

Like the chair joiners of old, Diffrient worked with full-size mock-ups. The difference was that he tested functionality rather than appearance. Often these early prototypes were very basic: plywood and metal assembled with wing nuts to allow adjustment. In his autobiography, Diffrient recounts how I. M. Pei, while visiting Diffrient's studio, spotted a test chair. "He thought it represented a final design, and before I could describe its purpose he complimented me on coming up with such a novel look for a chair." Pei's error is understandable because Diffrient's prototypes were carefully made; conversely, the final design often did resemble the test chair.

Diffrient's first self-adjusting office chair—named the Freedom Chair—was a commercial success. King's company sold a million chairs in the first decade. The Freedom Chair was followed by a conference room version, but it was the third chair, the World Chair, that was Diffrient's most fully evolved task chair. It was his last project—he was eighty when he designed it—and it distilled his ideas about seating to their essence. The World Chair "would contain all the fundamentals of comfort and support of a good work

World Chair
(Niels Diffrient)

chair," he wrote, "but be considerably more efficient and simple." He dispensed with the bulky counterbalanced recline mechanism and substituted a simple mechanical linkage; he described the chair as a scale, because it sensed the weight of the sitter and reacted accordingly. The back was plastic mesh, made of three sewn panels that, because they were fitted and did not stretch, provided effective lumbar support without any hardware. The simple frame was made of injection-molded glass-filled nylon, and with its pared-down design and lack of a mechanism the chair weighed only twenty-five pounds, half the weight of a typical task chair. That made it lighter to ship and, of course, used less material. As Diffrient pointed out, "No amount of recycling will equal using fewer resources in the first place."

The first time I sat on a World Chair, I noticed that the front edge of the seat was soft—there was no crossbar to exert upward pressure behind my knees. I adjusted the seat height by pressing a button under the right edge of the seat; a corresponding button on the left side controlled the seat depth. I moved the armrests by pulling them up or down. That was it. The plastic frame was slightly flexible, and when I leaned back, the comfortable chair leaned with me. Simplicity itself.

The light and graceful World Chair lacks the fussy, gadgety feeling of so many ergonomic task chairs today. It must be said that it also lacks the lyrical qualities of an Eames or a Wegner chair. Diffrient was strictly a "form follows function" man, and in that sense the World Chair is more like a Maclaren stroller than a high-design chair. It is not pretty, it is not seductive, it is just doing its job with, as its creator might have said, "unabashed purposefulness."*

A Rather Unsolvable Problem

Is the engineered task chair the ultimate chair? Not quite. Niels Diffrient devoted much of his working life to designing chairs, but even he was obliged to admit that sitting comfort was "a rather unsolvable problem." "Sitting is to be thought of as a compromise position," he observed, "since man in his natural habitat functions best when he is either erect and moving or supine and resting. Sitting is a cultural by-product. In many ways it counters the natural balance of physical man and his surroundings." He warned that "many of our physical ailments are by-products of sitting."

Today, there is mounting evidence that the effects of ex-tended sitting are indeed severe. A Canadian study that sam-pled 17,000 adults concluded that "greater daily time spent sitting in major activities is associated with elevated risks of mortality from all causes and from cardiovascular disease." An Australian study surveyed more than 200,000 men and women aged forty-five and older and asked them to record their total time sitting, whether working, at the dining table, watching television, playing computer games, driving a car, or traveling in a bus. The dramatic conclusion was that middle-aged people who sat for a total of more than eleven hours a day had a significantly greater chance of dying than

---

*This expression, which Diffrient quoted approvingly in his autobiography, originated with Alec Issigonis, the British automobile engineer who designed the Mini.

people who sat for four hours or less. Both studies concluded that regular physical exercise did not compensate for excessive sitting; the only antidote was to spend less time in chairs.

Mary Plumb Blade, the first woman appointed engineering professor at Cooper Union—in 1946—was not a chair designer but she studied sitting. "You can't sit in a chair comfortably for very long," she observed. "If you don't use muscles, you don't supply them with fresh blood; and without exercise, they start to atrophy immediately." She taught that movement was an integral part of sitting, and placed chairs in four categories: heavy chairs that were immobile, no matter the posture; light chairs that allowed movement, such as tilting back on two legs; chairs that became unstable when there was a poor match between chair and sitter; and mobile chairs that were designed to rock, swing, or swivel. Her point was that a chair is always part of a dynamic structure that includes the sitter's body.

What medical researchers call "incidental physical activity," that is, fidgeting, is positively associated with cardiorespiratory fitness. Chair designers have always known this. That's why Hans Wegner designed roomy easy chairs that permitted—and encouraged—movement. When Florence Knoll commissioned a lounge chair from Eero Saarinen, she told him, "I want a chair I can sit in sideways or any other way I want to sit in it." The result was the generously proportioned Womb Chair, which Saarinen described as "a great big cup-like shell into which you can curl up and pull up your legs."

There are chairs such as plane seats in which we feel like involuntary captives; on the other hand, there are chairs such as barstools on which we happily perch for long periods of time. Plumb would call a revolving barstool a mobile chair—it allows us to swing around and change positions, and to periodically redistribute our body weight between the stool, the footrest, and the bar counter. Another reason that bar-stools are comfortable is that we are almost standing. It has long been understood that sitting discomfort can be relieved by having a more open angle between thighs and torso, which may explain the current popularity of bar-height tables, or pub tables, in restaurants. One way to achieve this posture at work is to have taller desks with desk chairs similar to counter stools. Victorian clerks regularly worked at tall desks and, before computers, architects' drafting tables were waist-high and accompanied by tall stools. Pub desks, anyone?

Another work alternative is to not sit at all. Thomas Jefferson wrote standing up, so did Charles Dickens. Winston Churchill had a specially made lectern, and Ernest Hemingway simply placed his typewriter on a low bookcase. Vladimir Nabokov never learned to type, but he too worked standing up—at least part of the time. "I generally start the day at a lovely old-fashioned lectern I have in my study," he told an interviewer. "Later on, when I feel gravity nibbling at my calves, I settle down in a comfortable armchair along-side an ordinary writing desk; and finally, when gravity begins climbing up my spine, I lie down on a couch in a corner of my small study." This is a commonsense solution to the unsolvable problem. Despite the best efforts of human engineering there is no such thing as a perfect task chair. Instead of contrived chairs that are intended to make us sit upright, electrically powered desks that change heights, or silly contraptions such as treadmill desks, it would be simpler to sit sometimes, walk around sometimes, and, when we feel gravity nibbling, recline sometimes.

TWELVE

Our Time

I came across a news article about chairs. "A report released Tuesday by a team of researchers at the Brookings Institution has confirmed that the United States currently has enough chairs and there is no urgent need to produce new ones. Representing a five-year inquiry into the nation's seating availability and quality, the 85-page study of American homes, offices, dining establishments, public spaces, and patios has determined that, for now, the nation has 'plenty' of chairs and can get by just fine with the chairs it already possesses." The article elaborated this finding. "According to the report, chair production can cease entirely with no negative consequences for American consumers, as the many good chairs now on store shelves and available at garage sales are sufficient to satisfy the country's seating requirements for the immediate future. Though some citizens reportedly believe they require more chairs, the study found that most had not taken into full consideration the number of armchairs, folding chairs, Adirondack chairs, leather chairs, swivel chairs, and rocking chairs already in existence, not to mention all the beanbag chairs, wingback chairs, director's chairs, recliners, papasan chairs, and deck chairs."

This article appeared in *The Onion*, and like all good satire it contains more than a germ of truth. Why design more chairs when there are already so many different types available? Do we really need new chairs? It's not as if the old models have become obsolete. Although I don't powder my hair or wear buckled shoes, as the Founding Fathers did, I regularly sit on a Windsor chair, and my favorite wing chair is a replica of a mid-eighteenth-century design. My neighborhood bar is furnished with beat-up bentwood chairs—stools, side chairs, and upholstered No. A811Fs—which function perfectly well although their design is older than I am. All true, yet the history of the chair is a continuing chronicle of searching for new ways to sit and new furniture to sit on. Why?

First, chairs are affected by changes in technology and materials. The invention of upholstery in the eighteenth century changed the appearance of chairs and produced entirely new types: fauteuils, bergères, sofas. Steam-bending produced the Windsor chair and the bentwood chair. New materials such as tubular steel led to springy cantilever chairs; plywood and fiberglass allowed designers to conceive chair seats that were one-piece shells. Technical innovation was sometimes spurred by a search for economy, sometimes by a desire to discover a new solution to an old problem, and often chairmakers were simply along for the ride, exploiting technological advances in other fields. Like all modern artifacts, chairs reflect the shift from handwork to industrial production, meaning that as old techniques disappeared new ones were found to replace them: bentwood instead of carved wood, tubular steel instead of bentwood, shaped plywood instead of tubular steel, and plastic instead of plywood.

Second, chairs adapt to changing social conditions. The demand for greater informality in the placement of furniture in the eighteenth century encouraged the development of lighter, movable chairs. During the same period, the need for a comfortable place to sit alone for long periods while reading produced the easy chair. Leisurely sea voyages on ocean liners resulted in the recreational deck chair. When people smoked, the *chaise de fumeur* materialized; when people gave up smoking, the smoking chair—like the smoking jacket—became a distant memory. The advent of television accelerated the popularity of recliners. Similarly, the ergonomic task chair appeared just as people were spending more and more time sitting in front of their computers—at home as well as in the office. The tablet and the smartphone, whose users are not tied to desks, may herald the return of a chaise longue—or the advent of something new.*

Chairs are also affected by posture. It is a chicken-or-egg question, but on the whole I think posture usually comes first. The way we choose to sit is conditioned by culture, not by anatomy, and can change suddenly and unpredictably. How else to explain the emergence of the klismos, the advent of chair-sitting in Song dynasty China, the enthusiasm for rocking chairs in nineteenth-century America, or the popularity of chaises longues among twentieth-century modernists? What is certain is that when posture changes, the old chair no longer serves and a new one is needed. Conversely, if posture remains constant, the old models tend to endure. This may explain the longevity of the wing chair.

Lastly, chairs can be powerful symbols. In North American

---

*In 1984, Niels Diffrient, who once said, "The best chair is a bed," unveiled a horizontal workstation that consisted of a reclining chair and ottoman somewhat awkwardly combined with an IBM PC. He was three decades ahead of his time.

universities, departments are led—chaired—by chairper-
sons, endowed professorships are called chairs, and in many
institutions retiring faculty are honored with an actual
chair—usually a captain's chair or a Boston rocker, with the
university seal on the crest rail. The link between scholars
and chairs originated in the ancient Islamic world. Caliphs
appointed leading scholars to "chairs" in universities or ma-
drassas, the position so named because professors occupied
chairs whereas students sat on the floor.

The earliest symbolic chairs were those reserved for
royal, imperial, or religious leaders: St. Edward's corona-
tion chair in Westminster Abbey, the Dragon Throne of the
Chinese emperors, the Peacock Throne of the Persian shahs,
the Chair of St. Peter in the Vatican. The identification of
the occupant with the chair of state was so complete that
we still speak of "ascending the throne" or "usurping the
throne." The regal throne has parliamentary descendants.
The Speaker of the U.S. House of Representatives sits on the
most impressive chair in the chamber, although his chair
pales by comparison with that of the Speaker of the British
House of Commons, which is a canopy-topped, twelve-and-
a-half-foot-tall Gothic Revival chair that resembles a small
building.

The American president does not occupy a throne; he sits
behind a desk. In the past, the presidential desk chair was
passed down from incumbent to incumbent: William Howard Taft and Woodrow Wilson both sat on Theodore Roosevelt's stylish mahogany-and-rattan swivel desk chair; and
Franklin Delano Roosevelt made do with Herbert Hoover's
Colonial-style swivel chair, a cozy seat upholstered in a
patterned material. It was Truman, the Midwestern store-
keeper, who first used a large leather office chair, and subsequent presidents have followed his lead. A 2009 official

White House photograph shows the newly elected President Obama in the Oval Office trying out different desk chairs, while his predecessor's chair, a contemporary design in black leather with a tall headrest, stands forlornly to the side. Obama settled on a traditional—vaguely Georgian—executive chair with dark brown leather upholstery and curved mahogany arms. John F. Kennedy used an executive chair with a footstool, but the most memorable chair in the room was his rocking chair. It became such a potent symbol that when his succesor, Lyndon Johnson, redecorated the Oval Office, he acquired an identical rocker and pointedly sat on it during meetings.

An Aeron Chair would not suit the Oval Office, a reminder that furniture is generally a handmaiden of decor. When Frank Furness built the main library of the University of Pennsylvania in 1891, he furnished the main reading room with Thonet No. 18 café chairs, whose utilitarian character suited his architecture. (A hundred years later, when Robert Venturi and Denise Scott Brown restored the library, they chose red sack-back Windsor chairs—more comfortable but still in the spirit of this functionalist yet exuberant building.) In 1928, when the Swedish architect Erik Gunnar Asplund built the Stockholm Public Library, an example of Nordic classicism, he designed reading chairs with broad curved backs that recall klismos chairs. When Robert Adam built the Sackler Library in Oxford in 2001 in an austere classical style influenced by Asplund, he likewise designed a reading chair inspired by the Greek model. When Rem Koolhaas and Joshua Prince-Ramus furnished the Seattle Central Library, they chose seating to suit their building. Designed by the Belgian designer Maarten Van Severen, the desk chairs have plain metal legs and a molded black polyurethane seat and back that are pliable and slightly cushiony—industrial chic.

Chairs mirror taste as well as style. In the 1960s, for example, the papasan chair was all the rage. Introduced to the United States from Indonesia, this rattan easy chair consisted of a large bowl-shaped seat, three to four feet in diameter, fitted with a padded cushion. The seat was not attached to the base and could be rotated to be more or less reclined. Inexpensive and unconventional, the papasan was a favorite of college students. Today, there are so many used papasans for sale on the Internet that one writer called them "the Stair Masters of furniture." The beanbag chair was another 1960s fad. Unlike the papasan, which was a vernacular design, the beanbag was the work of three young Italian furniture designers. Called Sacco, the malleable pear-shaped bag filled with polystyrene pellets could accommodate a variety of postures, from upright to semireclined. Marketed as a *nonpoltrona* (nonchair), it was a graphic repudiation of mainstream taste. Beanbag chairs were especially good for listening to music, although getting up could be something of a struggle. We had a red Sacco in the late sixties. I also owned a pair of bell-bottom pants and a Nehru jacket. Eventually, the pants and the jacket stayed in the back of the closet; as for the chair, it died—the pellets must have got compressed, for the bag no longer kept its shape. While beanbag chairs are still sold today—in an astonishing variety of shapes and materials and in alarmingly large sizes—they seem like a throwback to an earlier time, a reflection of a particular countercultural moment.

An Artifact of Culture

Today, when I see a Sacco I think of Carnaby Street and Swinging London, just as a bergère, with its padded elbow

rests and carved gilded legs, brings to mind Madame de Pompadour, and a sack-back Windsor chair conjures up the Founding Fathers. Different times, different chairs. Perhaps one
reason that we create new kinds of chairs is because, in the
words of the design critic Ralph Caplan, "a chair is not an
artifact of service but an artifact of culture." That is why the
history of the chair is not evolutionary: a cabriole chair is not
"better" than a klismos, any more than an Eames lounge
chair is superior to a recamier. They are simply different—
they convey different meanings, carry different cultural mes-
sages, suit different tastes. "A chair is the first thing you need
when you don't really need anything," observed Caplan, "and
is therefore a peculiarly compelling symbol of civilization."
The way we choose to sit, and what we choose to sit on, says
a lot about us: our values, our tastes, the things we hold
dear.

If a chair can represent an epoch, what chair will the
future consider emblematic of *our* time? An airplane seat?
Business-class seats on transatlantic flights have improved
greatly since the days when they resembled overstuffed recliners, but economy seats have, if anything, degenerated as
space constraints have made them leaner and meaner. We
spend a lot of time in cars. Modern car seats have as many
controls as ergonomic task chairs, although the fashion for
bucket seats has constrained motility to an excessive degree.
A recent ride in the backseat of a vintage Packard convinced
me that there is nothing like sitting on a wide couch with
freedom to move and plenty of leg room for real comfort.

If not a plane or car seat, what about a designer chair?
Few companies have produced as many modern classics as
Knoll, the company founded by Hans and Florence Knoll in
1938. I visit the Knoll Museum, which adjoins the company's
manufacturing plant in East Greenville, Pennsylvania.

"Museum" makes it sound too grand; it is more like a showroom with some seventy of the company's chairs on the floor. What makes this museum better than any design collection I've ever visited is that you are allowed to sit on the chairs.

The oldest design in the museum is Mies van der Rohe's 1927 cantilever MR10, his first tubular chair.* It turns out to be reason-

*Tugendhat Chair
(Ludwig Mies van der Rohe
and Lilly Reich)*

ably comfortable, with a pleasant wicker seat and wicker-wrapped arms. Two years later Mies produced the Barcelona Chair; roomy, although the slumped position would be wearying over time, and since there are no arms, getting up is awkward. Mies's Tugendhat Chair, likewise designed with Lilly Reich about the same time, avoids that problem. Reich was an experienced designer, having worked with Josef Hoffman on several chairs. The Tugendhat Chair, a wide cantilever lounge chair with a tufted seat and well-padded arms, is less celebrated than either the MR10 or the Barcelona, but I would prefer it if I were sitting down to read a book. Like the MR10, it is extremely resilient—a bouncy chair. I'd always admired Marcel Breuer's handsome B35 lounge chair of that same era, but I had never sat on it, and I'm disappointed. Although both the seat and the arms are separately cantilevered there is not much resilience, and the top bar cuts into my back. Next I try Breuer's molded plywood chaise longue, influenced by Aalto and produced in England

---

*Over the years, Knoll acquired the rights to many Mies and Breuer chairs.

in the 1930s. It is more flexible, although unlike Dr. Pascaud's *Sur-repos* the confining arms do not swing open, so getting in and out requires ungraceful acrobatics. Not pleasant at all.

A small chair catches my eye. Upholstered in bright red hopsack, it looks like a furry amoeba. It's the 1940 Museum of Modern Art competition-winner designed by Saarinen and Eames; I'm not sure what it's doing here, since this reproduction is manufactured by Vitra, a Swiss company. When I sit on it, the laminated wood is slightly springy and the thinly padded upholstery provides firm support. A very nice chair, if somewhat small for me. There are several other Saarinen chairs on the floor. The classic Tulip Chair, with its wineglass base and fiberglass seat, is okay, although it strikes me as less than ideal for dining since it can't be pulled up to the table—it swivels instead. Yet it remains a popular chair. So does the deceptively simple 1950 Model 71 executive armchair, which was the chair that Niels Diffrient worked on as a Cranbrook student. Charles Eames judged the Model 71 to be Saarinen's "best functional piece." Sitting in it I can see why. "Timeless classic" is a hackneyed term, but the Model 71 qualifies.

A nearby executive desk chair is so low-key I almost pass it by. Although the armrests are plastic, the plushy tufted leather looks inviting so I sit down. In some indefinable way, I feel immediately at home—a matter of the generous dimensions, a soft seat, and the cozy sense of being contained. The chair was designed by Charles Pollock in the 1960s, and is said to have taken him five years. "I mean, you just fiddle with it forever and run back and forth to the factory and talk to Mrs. Knoll forever until finally it just gels," he told an interviewer. Pollock's fiddling produced a deceptively sophisticated design. The polished metal rim, which looks like a bumper rail, is actually an aluminum extrusion that

forms the structure of the chair as
well as providing a place to attach
the upholstery and the back
panel. What dates the design are
the minimal controls—only chair
height and tilt tension can be
adjusted—but this chair doesn't
need more.

The 40/4 stacking chair (not
manufactured by Knoll) was another innovative chair that appeared in 1963. Like Pollock, the
designer David Rowland worked

*Executive chair
(Charles Pollock)*

slowly and it took him eight years to complete the chair,
which consisted of a frame of very thin bent steel rods supporting a contoured seat and a back made out of vinyl-
coated sheet metal. The light chair—fourteen pounds—was
intended to be a temporary seat that could be stored when
not in use. The 40/4's unique feature was that forty of them
could be stacked in only four feet—hence the name. Although
intended as a temporary seat, it was comfortable and elegant
enough to be used in recital halls and restaurants. Variants
included armchairs, lounge chairs, writing-arm chairs, barstools, and outdoor chairs, with metal, wood, plastic, or
padded seats. The 40/4 replaced the Eames shell chair as the
iconic modern chair and became the bestselling designer
chair of that epoch.*

The 1950s and '60s were exceptional decades in American furniture design. Like Saarinen's Model 71 and Pollock's

---

*More than 8 million 40/4 chairs have been sold since its debut. In 1981, 40/4s
filled Westminster Cathedral for Princess Diana's wedding.

*40/4 stacking chair
(David Rowland)*

executive chair, Rowland's stacking chair is still in production and still popular. But these chairs can hardly be called emblematic of our time, being more than half a century old. There are more recent chairs displayed in the Knoll Museum, but they are chairs whose time has come and gone: a fragile retro barrel chair designed by Richard Meier in 1982; an equally uncomfortable but more colorful armchair by Ettore Sottsass of the Italian design group Memphis, and three plywood side chairs by Robert Venturi that are fun to look at but definitely not fun to sit on. All are a reminder that nothing ages as quickly as a contrived chair.

The Sottsass and Venturi chairs are emblematic of the brief postmodern episode, but like Hector Guimard's sinuous Art Nouveau furniture of the fin de siècle they are too idiosyncratic to have a long life. A similar fate may befall a line of chairs that Frank Gehry designed for Knoll in 1990. They are constructed entirely of laminated maple veneer strips less than a quarter-inch thick, bent into curves and glued together. The playful chairs, which recall bushel baskets, are extremely light, and the flexible material makes them comfortable to sit on. The chairs have some of the easygoing charm of a deck chair, although their laid-back casualness is deceptive. These are luxury products—you could get a dozen 40/4s for the price of a single Gehry side chair. But who can tell what the future holds? When Thonet stopped manufacturing tubular steel furniture in the late

1930s, few would have anticipated that the Wassily Chair would become the iconic chair of early modernism. It is quite possible that at some future date, the bushel-basket chairs will be judged to be the perfect emblems of our extravagant age.

Flip-Flops

I asked John Dunnigan what he thought would qualify as the emblematic chair of our time. In addition to being an experienced chairmaker, John heads the furniture design department at the Rhode Island School of Design. He is knowledgeable about the history of chairs and I knew he would have an interesting opinion.

Of course one has to first acknowledge that most of the chairs we think of as emblematic of their time were considered that in retrospect, which points out the difficulty of anyone doing that now for our time. And we know that art history and criticism are not impartial. Having said that, as strong as the celebrity designer chair market has been over the last thirty years, the chair that is most representative in my opinion is unquestionably the anonymous monobloc polypropylene chair. I've been fascinated by this chair for many years since I bought my first one at a supermarket in the 1980s. Versions of it are produced by companies around the world. It's a technical tour de force, a marketing miracle, a cultural phenomenon, and potentially an environmental disaster, which could be emblematic of our time, too.

The monobloc (meaning one-piece) chair to which Dunnigan was referring, sometimes called a resin chair, is the ubiquitous white plastic patio chair that sells for as little as ten dollars—your local supermarket probably has stacks of them.

The Milanese journalist Marco Velardi, who edits *Apartamento*, an offbeat "everyday life interiors magazine," gave the same answer when I asked him about today's emblematic chair.

Monobloc plastic patio chair

"It's not easy to define a chair of our time, but the first thing that came to my mind was a plastic chair. If I think of my childhood and the times I've traveled and visited places, and with that I don't mean fancy places that are trying to be fashionable or trendy, I think of plastic chairs, in their many shapes, simple or more refined, in cafés, airports, hospitals, offices, apartments." My friend Andrew Morrison, who has designed several chairs for Knoll, as well as a long-lived open-plan office system, agreed. "The plastic chair is our major contribution to chair design," he told me. "It got rid of all those damn joints. Whenever I see a television report about a terrorist bombing in the Middle East there are intact plastic chairs strewn all over the place. Wooden chairs would never survive the blast, they'd be splintered to pieces." In the early 1960s, freshly graduated from Pratt Institute, Andrew, who already had a chair in production, proposed a one-piece fiberglass chair to Knoll. "Florence Knoll told me, 'It's not for us,'" he recalls. "At that point injection-molded chairs didn't exist," he said. "There were only two large injection machines in the United States, and they were making dash-boards for Ford."

The two first commercially produced one-piece plastic chairs appeared only a few years later, designed by Helmut Bätzner in Germany and Vico Magistretti in Italy. The challenge in making a chair out of thin plastic is not the seat—the Eameses had solved that problem—but the legs, which need to be rigid. Bätzner stiffened the legs by giving them an L-shaped cross-section; Magistretti used an S shape. The stacking side chairs were molded out of one piece of fiberglass-reinforced polyester, but they were relatively costly to manufacture and did not find a large market. It would be another two decades before the familiar mass-produced plastic patio chair arrived, made possible by advances in injection technology using cheap polypropylene rather than expensive fiberglass-reinforced polyester. The first injected plastic products were buckets, housewares, and automobile parts. It is unclear exactly who applied this technology to a one-piece chair—it may have been a French company.* In any case, it was sometime in the mid-1980s, and the chair was definitely the brainchild of a plastics manufacturer, not a traditional furniture company.

The most common version of the monobloc chair has arms that extend around the rear to form a backrest and support back splats. In most chairs, these splats—fan-shaped, or otherwise patterned—are the chair's only ornamental feature. Splats are traditional, but the monobloc is not an offshoot of any particular chair—this is not a Kubleresque "replica." The design is almost entirely dictated by the man-

---

*The British Polyprop Chair, which appeared in 1963, was the first chair made of injected polypropylene, although only the one-piece seat and back was plastic; the legs were metal.

ufacturing process and the desire to minimize material. The plastic is thin—less than ¼ inch—and the arms and legs have ribs and L-shaped profiles to provide stiffness. The chair is so light that it can be stacked in piles of twenty or more. White is the most common color, but forest green and dark brown are also popular. And the material resists the elements. Resists all too well: broken plastic chairs litter the landscape.

The fabrication process for a monobloc chair is entirely automated and takes place inside a large machine the size of a tour bus. About five pounds of plastic pellets are mixed with hardener, dye, and other additives, heated to 430°F, and the molten material is injected into a mold under extremely high pressure. After being cooled, the two-piece mold opens and a robot arm removes the completed chair; no finishing or handwork is required. The whole process, from pellets to completed chair, takes less than a minute. Since the raw material is relatively inexpensive, the production cost is extremely low.

The chief investment for a monobloc chair manufacturer, other than the injection-molding machine itself, is the precision mold. To pay for the mold it is necessary to produce hundreds of thousands of identical chairs (no variation is possible except color). Over time the mold loses accuracy and must be replaced. Secondhand molds are sold to less demanding producers in the Third World, and thus the monobloc chair has spread around the globe. A Flickr website called "Those White Plastic Chairs" contains more than a thousand images: solitary chairs and chairs massed in groups, chairs in towns and chairs on the beach, chairs left on snowy city streets to reserve parking spaces. There are photographs of plastic chairs occupied by the faithful at the Wailing Wall, ebola patients in a Liberian clinic, and tired American marines in Iraq. The images include plastic chairs converted into low-cost wheelchairs, and broken chairs with jury-rigged metal legs. Plastic chairs are everywhere—on a condominium balcony in Vancouver, in a Venetian trattoria, a sidewalk eatery in Phnom Penh, an outdoor barbershop in Lagos, or a favela in Rio. Monoblocs are the furniture equivalent of rubber flip-flops.

The global monobloc represents the culmination of the dream of a universal mass-produced chair that began with Thonet and was pursued by the Bauhaus designers. With its absence of details—no joints, as Morrison pointed out—it fulfills Charles Eames's criterion for a chair that "would have in its appearance the essence of the method that produced it." The monobloc is light, portable, stackable, waterproof, easy to clean, and, of course, extremely cheap. We have seen how, over the years, chairs have been affected by changes in production: the shift from carpentry to cabinetmaking, from workshop to factory, and from factory to assembly line. Automated plastic injection goes one step further, turning the chair into a mass-market commodity.

Despite its huge success—it is undoubtedly the most common chair on the planet—the monobloc has not enjoyed the social acceptance of rubber sandals; it is more likely to be reviled or, at least, ignored. A deck chair on the beach is charming; a plastic chair on the beach is an intrusive piece of flotsam. Most people find plastic chairs tacky. That's undoubtedly the reason that the City of New York provides Parisian folding chairs rather than monoblocs in Bryant Park and in the pedestrianized parts of Broadway.* The black polyurethane chairs in the Seattle Central Library are stylish in a way that monobloc chairs could never hope to

---

*The stylish wood-and-metal folding bistro chair is another nineteenth-century chair that has endured—it was patented in 1889.

be. Of course, the Seattle library chairs cost about seven hundred dollars each. The low price of the monobloc precludes any sense of status—this is just a cheap throwaway. When Le Corbusier furnished his interiors with Thonet café chairs in the 1920s, he was being provocative, placing a commercial product in a residential setting. But since the ubiquitous monobloc is already at home everywhere, a monobloc in the living room has all the cachet of a plastic dairy crate.

The monobloc has another disadvantage—at least as far as the design world is concerned. Ever since the 1920s, advances in chair design have been linked to individuals: Breuer, Aalto, the Eameses, Saarinen, Jacobsen, Rowland. The cantilever chair, the butterfly chair, the beanbag chair, even the recliner, have a design pedigree. The monobloc, on the other hand, is a renegade. Although mass-produced, it is a throwback to anonymous chairs like the Windsor and the rocker. Like them, it simply appeared, not out of the folkish blue, but out of a global industrial murk.

Unlike the Windsor chair, however, the generic monobloc is definitely not a paragon of design. The shiny plastic finish is unpleasant to the touch, sticky to sit on for any length of time, and its color fades in sunlight. At five pounds, the chair is too light. It's all very well for a folding lawn chair to be light—that is the trade-off we accept for its portability—but we expect a stationary chair to feel more substantial. In addition, the thin unreinforced plastic is weak. Flexibility in a chair is not a bad thing—it can actually add to comfort—but the cheapest monoblocs are notoriously frail. "The chairs seem very flimsy, the back rails bend when you lean against the back. They feel unstable," reads a typical online customer complaint. "The chairs are so weak, I am afraid to let my guests sit in them," reads another. A chair should lend the sitter a measure of dignity, but the monobloc is an object of ridicule. "The Tupperware container of a lard-rumped universe," a *Washington Post* reporter called it. If a chair is a symbol of civilization, as Ralph Caplan claimed, then the monobloc is a sad reflection of a global consumer society that is oblivious of the past, aims for the lowest common denominator, and is little concerned with long-term quality.

What would a well-made, well-designed monobloc look like? One of the first designers to turn his attention to this question was Jasper Morrison (no relation), a British industrial designer. Morrison's low-key approach to design tends to favor subtle improvements over radically new forms. This is evident in the chairs he has designed. A beechwood dining chair, for example, looks like something from a Thonet catalog of the 1930s, until you realize that the seat and backrest are not laminated wood but plastic—more flexible than wood. A café chair recalls a traditional woven-cane brasserie chair, except that the seat is molded from reclaimed wood and plastic. He describes a metal-and-plastic stacking chair as a "descendant" of the 40/4. Evidently, Morrison is prepared to learn from the past. This attitude is unusual among contemporary designers and reminds me of Kaare Klint's axiom: "All the problems are not new, and several of them have been solved before."

Morrison's monobloc, called the Air-Chair, is so low-key it is almost banal. With four unbraced tubular legs, a tubular frame, and a solid seat and back, the chair resembles a child's drawing of a chair. Some designers give plastic chairs paper-thin profiles; not Morrison—his side chair is distinctly chunky, with squarish proportions and rounded edges. The plastic has a matte, slightly textured finish and comes in eight colors: black, white, several pastel hues, a cheerful orange, and a rather alarming fuchsia. Unlike beechwood and woven cane, plastic is not inherently attractive, yet Morrison

Air-Chair
(Jasper Morrison)

manages to tease something pleasing out of this unpromising material. An oblong carry handle cut into the seat reminds me of Wagner's Postsparkasse stool and doubles as a drain when the chair is left outside. The shaped seat is comfortable and the chair feels rock solid. The plastic is reinforced with fiberglass, which makes it stronger, and there is more material—this chair is twice as heavy as a generic monobloc. Yet when I lift it, perhaps because it is so sturdy, it feels surprisingly light.

The Air-Chair has a curious quality for a designer chair—it doesn't draw attention to itself. In that sense, it's more like an everyday object such as a push broom or a clay flower pot. Such artifacts, as Morrison has observed, are neither handmade nor unique, and their designers are unknown. Yet they have a curious kind of authority. This is also true of well-designed industrial products. When we look at a circular Honeywell thermostat, we don't think, "Oh yes, Henry Dreyfuss designed that," we simply want to adjust the room temperature, and the familiar, self-explanatory dial helps us to do the job. When we want to sit down, we pull up an Air-Chair and it does its job, too.

Morrison's monobloc costs more than a standard plastic patio chair. "The price of a monobloc chair depends on the technology used and the volume of production," he explained in an e-mail. "The cheaper variety are made in millions and tend to be single-wall moldings with reinforcement ribs, while the more expensive (usually designer versions) tend to make use of a technology called gas injection (hence the name Air-Chair), which blows the plastic against the mold in areas where the sections need to be tubular for structural reasons, creating something like a bone structure of hollowed-out tubes. The molding is more complicated and the mold cost is higher, the cycle time is longer, the chairs use more plastic but are much stronger." The Air-Chair, which was designed in 1999, was one of the first monoblocs to use the new technology. Its homogenous tubular structure wouldn't make sense with any other manufacturing technique.

The stacking Air-Chair was intended for outdoor use on café terraces, but is handsome enough to be used indoors as library and cafeteria seating, or even as a dining chair at home—unexpected settings for a plastic chair. Like its throw-away monobloc cousin, it is yet another addition to the chair universe. There is surely room for an everyday chair that can be used indoors and out, that is not a precious artifact, and that will give years of service. Not that plastic chairs will replace the other kind. If history teaches anything, it is that the chair is never merely—or only—a tool for sitting. The rightness of a chair for its job is only one of its many indefinable pleasures, and the variety of these pleasures precludes a single solution. Remember Voltaire's necessity of frills.

The future of the chair probably lies somewhere between the ergonomic task chair and the improved gas-injected monobloc. That is, between a chair that can adapt to the widest possible range of postures and body sizes, and an inexpensive chair for the masses. Yet that future is uncertain, because chair design is not a science. Important discoveries are made and forgotten. Lumbar support was invented by the Chinese and informed chairmaking in Georgian England, yet the early modernist designers chose to ignore this feature in favor of straight backs and right-angled geometry. Sprung upholstery can be a great aid to sitting comfort, yet it has fallen out of favor in recent years. We spend a lot of time in adjustable chairs—in cars and on planes—but with the exception of the much-maligned recliner, we rarely use adjustable chairs at home. Currently, the mesh task chair represents the most advanced solution to healthful sitting, yet domestic furniture has generally resisted incorporating similar ergonomic features.

This is hardly the end of the story. A hundred years from now we'll no doubt be using plastic chairs of some sort, but we'll still have Adirondack chairs at the cottage—or whatever we will call our country hideaways. We'll also be sitting on as-yet-unimagined chairs made out of as-yet-unimagined materials. Chairs will likely accompany space colonists on their travels. They may be some sort of inflatable contraptions, or simply aluminum lawn chairs. The chair endures, even as it never ceases to change.

NOTES ON SOURCES

1. A Tool for Sitting

A detailed description of François Boucher's *Le déjeuner* is contained in *What Great Paintings Say: Volume 2* (Taschen, 2003) by Rose-Marie and Rainer Hagen. George Kubler's penetrating study is *The Shape of Time: Remarks on the History of Things* (Yale University Press, 1962). Christopher Alexander's observation on furniture is from *A Pattern Language: Towns, Buildings, Construction* (Oxford University Press, 1977).

2. If You Sit on It, Can It Still Be Art?

Jean-François Oeben's mechanical dressing table is discussed by André Boutemy in "Les Table-Coiffeuses de Jean-François Oeben," *Bulletin de la Société de l'histoire de l'art français* (1962). Details of Émilie du Châtelet and Voltaire's life at Cirey are vividly described by Nancy Mitford in *Voltaire in Love* (E. P. Dutton, 1985). Françoise de Graffigny's description of Madame du Châtelet's rooms is from *Françoise de Graffigny: Choix de Lettres*, English Showalter, ed. (Voltaire Foundation, 2001). Showalter's "Graffigny at Cirey: A Fraud Exposed," *French Forum* 21 (January 1996), is also revealing. John Summerson's wise observation on ornament is from "The Mischievous Analogy" in *Heavenly Mansions: And Other Essays on Architecture* (W. W. Norton, 1963). I first explored the subject of ornament in "Homo Ornarens," an essay in *Designed for Delight: Alternative Aspects of Twentieth-Century Decorative Arts*, Martin Eidelberg, ed. (Flammarion, 1997), which accompanied an exhibition at Montreal's Musée des arts décoratifs. I wrote about John Dunnigan's furniture in the Arts &

Leisure section of *The New York Times* (May 5, 1991). Quotes from Dunnigan are based on personal conversations and are also drawn from *John Dunnigan Furniture Maker* (Peter Joseph Gallery, 1991), an interview with Dunnigan in Bebe Pritam Johnson and Warren Eames Johnson's *Speaking of Furniture: Conversations with 14 American Masters* (Artist Book Foundation, 2013), and Dunnigan's essay in *Under Cover: Some Thoughts on Upholstered Furniture*, an exhibition catalogue (Gallery NAGA, Boston, 2005).

3. Sitting Up

Gordon W. Hewes's classic study "The Anthropology of Posture" appeared in *Scientific American* (February 1957) and was originally published as "World Distribution of Certain Postural Habits" in *American Anthropologist*, vol. 2, no. 1, part 1 (April 1955). G.M.A. Richter's authoritative *The Furniture of the Greeks, Etruscans and Romans* (Phaidon Press, 1966) provides much useful information. The Bernard Rudofsky quote is from *Behind the Picture Window* (Oxford University Press, 1955). The Chinese adoption of the chair is described in several scholarly works: C. P. FitzGerald's *Barbarian Beds: The Origin of the Chair in China* (Cresset Press, 1965); Sarah Handler's *Austere Luminosity of Chinese Classical Furniture* (University of California Press, 2001); and George N. Kates's pioneering *Chinese Household Furniture* (Harper & Brothers, 1948). The French diplomat's 1795 visit to Peking is quoted by Fernand Braudel in *The Structures of Everyday Life: The Limits of the Possible*, Siân Reynolds, trans. (Harper & Row, 1981), which is also the source of the other Braudel quotes. Nicolas Andry's *Orthopaedia* (J. B. Lippincott, 1961) is a facsimile edition of the first English translation, which was published in London in 1743, two years after it appeared in Paris. Ellen Davis Kelly's observation on posture is from *Teaching Posture and Body Mechanics* (Ronald Press, 1949). The research of Drs. Staffel and Strasser is discussed by Edward H. Bradford and Robert W. Lovett in *Treatise on Orthopedic Surgery* (William Wood, 1899). Bengt Åkerblom documents his research in *Standing and Sitting Posture, with Special Reference to the Construction of Chairs*, Ann Synge, trans. (A.B. Nordiska Bokhandlen, 1948). Paul Branton's evocative description of the dynamics of sitting is from *The Comfort of Easy Chairs* (Furniture Industry Research Association, 1966).

4. A Chair on the Side

Cycladic sculpture is discussed by Pat Getz-Preziosi in *Early Cycladic Sculpture: An Introduction* (J. Paul Getty Museum, 1994) and by Joan R. Mertins in "Some Long Thoughts on Early Cycladic Sculpture," *Metropoli-*

tan Museum Journal 33 (1998). I gleaned information on Roman chairs from G.M.A. Richter's *The Furniture of the Greeks, Etruscans and Romans* and Roger B. Ulrich's *Roman Woodworking* (Yale University Press, 2007). The seating arrangement of the trial of Jean II, Duke of Alençon, is detailed in S. H. Cuttler, "A Report to Sir John Fastolf on the Trial of Jean, Duke of Alençon," *The English Historical Review*, vol. 96, no. 381 (October 1981). The Braudel quote is from *The Structures of Everyday Life*. Seventeenth-century chairs are discussed by John Gloag in *The Englishman's Chair: Origins, Design, and Social History of Seat Furniture in England* (George Allen & Unwin, 1964), which remains a useful reference. Vincent Scully's vivid description of the cabriole chair is from *New World Visions of Household Gods & Sacred Places: American Art and the Metropolitan Museum of Art 1650–1914* (Little, Brown, 1988).

5. A Golden Age

I came across the Ham House "sleeping chayres" in *The English Chair: Its History and Evolution* (M. Harris & Sons, 1937), and they are also described by John Gloag in *A Social History of Furniture Design: From B.C. 1300 to A.D. 1960* (Bonanza Books, 1966). I have referred to A. Hepplewhite & Co., *The Cabinet Maker and Upholsterers Guide* (I. & J. Taylor, 1794), and Thomas Chippendale, *The Gentleman and Cabinet Maker's Director* (1754). Christopher Gilbert's exemplary biography, *The Life and Work of Thomas Chippendale* (Studio Vista, 1978), is a useful source. The story of Chippendale's smuggling is recounted by Edward T. Joy in "Chippendale in Trouble at the Customs," *Country Life* 110 (August 24, 1951). I leaned heavily on Bill G. B. Pallot's first-rate *The Art of the Chair in Eighteenth-Century France* (ACR-Gismondi Editeurs, 1989), and also drew on Charles Saumarez Smith's *Eighteenth-Century Decoration: Design and the Domestic Interior in England* (Harry N. Abrams, 1993) and John Whitehead's *The French Interior: In the Eighteenth Century* (Dutton Studio Books, 1992). The Peter Thornton quote is from his penetrating study, *Authentic Decor: The Domestic Interior, 1620–1920* (Viking, 1984).

6. Sack-backs and Rockers

Luke Vincent Lockwood's *Colonial Furniture in America* (Charles Scribner's Sons, 1921) is a valuable reference to the period. The Richard L. Bushman quote is from *The Refinement of America: Persons, Houses, Cities* (Alfred A. Knopf, 1992). For a description of the furniture at Mount Vernon see Helen Maggs Fede's detailed *Washington Furniture at Mount Vernon* (Mount Vernon Ladies' Association of the Union, 1966), Margaret Van

Cott's "Thomas Burling of New York City, Exponent of the New Republic Style," *Furniture History* 37 (2001), and Allan Greenberg's *George Washington, Architect* (Andreas Papadakis, 1999). I also consulted Thomas H. Ormsbee's *The Windsor Chair* (Hearthside Press, 1962) and Nancy Goyne Evans's exhaustive *American Windsor Furniture: Specialized Forms* (Hudson Hills Press, 1997). The Philip Schaff quote is from *America: Its Political, Social and Religious Character* (Harvard University Press, 1961; originally published in 1854).

7. The Henry Ford of Chairs

Christopher Wilk's *Thonet: 150 Years of Furniture* (Barron's, 1980) is essential reading. *Thonet Bentwood & Other Furniture: The 1904 Illustrated Catalog* (Dover Publications, 1980) is a useful source of information on various Thonet products. I also consulted Alexander von Vegesack's *Thonet: Classic Furniture in Bent Wood and Tubular Steel* (Rizzoli, 1996), Hans H. Buchwald's *Form from Process: The Thonet Chair,* an exhibition catalogue (Carpenter Center for the Visual Arts, Harvard University, 1967), and Eve B. Ottillinger's *Gebrüder Thonet: Möbel aus gebogenem Holz* (Böhlau Verlag, 2003).

8. By Design

The Vitra Design Museum's quote on the Wassily Chair is from its website's "100 Masterpieces." The Museum of Modern Art quote is from Barry Bergdoll and Leah Dickerson's *Bauhaus, 1919–1933: Workshops for Modernity* (Museum of Modern Art, 2009). Philip Johnson described his Barcelona Chairs in "The Seven Crutches of Modern Architecture" in *Writings* (Oxford University Press, 1979). My old professor Peter Collins's observation on the Rietveld chair is from "Furniture Givers as Form Givers: Is Design an All-Encompassing Skill?" *Progressive Architecture* (March 1963). For information on Marcel Breuer's furniture, I consulted Christopher Wilk's *Marcel Breuer: Furniture and Interiors* (Museum of Modern Art, 1981) and *Modernism: Designing a New World,* Christopher Wilk, ed. (V & A Publications, 2006). The best single source on Alvar Aalto's chairs is *Alvar Aalto Furniture,* Juhani Pallasmaa, ed. (MIT Press, 1984). Aalto's sanatorium furniture is discussed in "The Paimio Interiors" by Kaarina Mikonranta in *Alvar Aalto Architect, Volume 5, Paimio Sanatorium, 1929–33* (Alvar Aalto Foundation, 2014). The *Architectural Review* quote is from "Standard Wooden Furniture at the Finnish Exhibition," *Architectural Review* 74 (December 1, 1933). Saarinen and Eames's collaboration at Cranbrook is described by R. Craig Miller in "Interior Design and Furniture" in *Design in America: The Cranbrook Vision 1925–1950* (Harry N. Abrams, 1984). Information on the Eames molded plywood chairs is from Christopher Wilk's "Furnishing the Future: Bent Mood and Metal Furniture, 1925–46" in *Bent Wood and Metal Furniture: 1850–1946*, Derek E. Ostergard, ed. (University of Washington Press, 1987). I also depended on Pat Kirkham's *Charles and Ray Eames: Designers of the Twentieth Century* (MIT Press, 1995). The long quote by Charles Eames about the plywood shell chair is from John Neuhart, Marilyn Neuhart, and Ray Eames, *Eames Design: The Work of the Office of Charles and Ray Eames* (Harry N. Abrams, 1989).

9. Great Dane

Wegner's obituary, "Hans Wegner Dies at 92; Danish Furniture Designer," appeared in *The New York Times* (February 6, 2007). The chief source of the Wegner quotes is a comprehensive book on his life and work published on the occasion of the centenary of his birth: Christian Holmsted Olesen's *Wegner: Just One Good Chair*, Mark Mussari, trans. (Hatje Cantz, 2014). Another useful source is Jens Bernsen's short monograph *Hans J. Wegner* (Danish Design Center, 2001). David Pye's *The Nature and Art of Workmanship* (Cambium Press, 1968) is an exceptional meditation on the subject. The first American coverage of Danish Modern furniture was "Danish Furniture: Old Hands Give Shape to New Ideas," *Interiors* (February 1950). The Danish Modern movement is described in Per H. Hansen's "The Construction of a Brand: The Case of Danish Design, 1930–1970" (unpublished paper, EBHA-Conference, Barcelona, September 2004), Andrew Hollingsworth's *Danish Modern* (Gibbs Smith, 2008), and *Contemporary Danish Design*, Arne Karlsen et al., eds. (Danish Society of Arts and Crafts and Industrial Design, 1960). The 1960 Metropolitan Museum show was reviewed by Sanka Knox, "Long-Awaited Museum Show Opens," *The New York Times* (October 15, 1960).

10. Fold and Knockdown, Swing and Roll

Information on the Chinese folding chair is from *Austere Luminosity of Chinese Classical Furniture*. Nicholas A. Brawer's *British Campaign Furniture: Elegance Under Canvas, 1740–1914* (Harry N. Abrams, 2001) is essential reading on the subject. The IKEA quote is from Lauren Collins, "House Perfect" (*The New Yorker*, October 3, 2011). Although I don't agree with all of Galen Cranz's conclusions, *The Chair: Rethinking Culture, Body, and Design* (W. W. Norton, 1998) is a rare example of a scholarly treatment of the subject. The quote about Indian *jhoolas* is from Kusum Choppra's *Beyond Diamond Rings* (Pustak Mahal, 2010). Eighteenth-century swings are discussed by Donald Posner in "The Swinging Women of Watteau and Fragonard," *The Art Bulletin*, vol. 64, no. 1 (March 1982). The description of

Oeben's mechanical chair is included in Rosemarie Stratmann's "Design and Mechanisms in the Furniture of Jean-François Oeben," *Furniture History* 9 (1973). The description of Grollier's wheelchair is from Gaspard Grollier de Servière, *Recueil d'ouvrages curieux de mathématique et mécanique, ou description du cabinet de monsieur Grollier de Servière* (C. A. Jombert, 1751). Merlin and his inventions are described in *John Joseph Merlin: The Ingenious Mechanick* (Greater London Council, 1985).

ii. Human Engineering

The prewar saga of Anton Lorenz and the cantilever chair is described in detail by Otakar Máčel in "Avant-Garde Design and the Law: Litigation over the Cantilever Chair," *Journal of Design History*, vol. 3, nos. 2/3 (1990), and in Christopher Wilk's *Marcel Breuer: Furniture and Interiors*. Lorenz's later work in America on the recliner has received less attention, and I am indebted to Edward Tenner's *Our Own Devices: The Past and Future of Body Technology* (Alfred A. Knopf, 2003). The origin of the Aeron Chair is recounted by Cliff Kuang in "The Secret History of the Aeron Chair," *Slate* (posted November 5, 2012). Seth Stevenson's comments on the limitations of the adjustable task chair are from "A Search for the Best Desk Chair," *Slate* (posted December 6, 2005). Diffrient's observation about the limitations of ergonomic chairs is from an interview with Martin C. Pedersen, "Niels Diffrient: A Tribute in Conversation," *Metropolis* (posted June 17, 2013). The Humanscale manual quoted is Niels Diffrient, Alvin R. Tilley, and Joan C. Bardagly, *Humanscale 1/2/3: Sizes of People, Seating Considerations, Requirements for the Handicapped and Elderly* (MIT Press, 1974). Diffrient's autobiography, *Confessions of a Generalist* (Generalist Ink, 2012), contains much useful information about furniture design and is a revealing window into the mind of the noted industrial designer. The Diffrient quote about working with Saarinen is contained in Jayne Merkel's *Eero Saarinen* (Phaidon Press, 2005). The Diffrient observation about airplane seats is from "Objective Performance, Comfort Indicators and Compromises" in *Chair: The Current State of the Art, with the How, the Why, and the What of It*, Peter Bradford and Barbara Prete, eds. (Thomas Y. Crowell, 1978). Diffrient's explanation of his method of designing chairs is from a video interview on the Humanscale website. Diffrient's comment about the insoluble problem of the chair is from his "Objective Performance, Comfort Indicators and Compromises." The Canadian study of sitting ailments is P. T. Katzmarzyk et al., "Sitting Time and Mortality from All Causes, Cardiovascular Disease, and Cancer," *Medicine & Science in Sports & Exercise*, vol. 41, no. 5 (May 2009); the Australian study is Hidde P. van der Plogge et al., "Sitting Time and All-Cause Mortality Risk in 222,497 Australian Adults," *Archives of Internal Medicine* (March 26, 2012). Mary

Plumb Blade is quoted from "Physical Forces and Damages, Your Sitting Behavior, Move" in *Chair*. Florence Knoll and Eero Saarinen's comments about the Womb Chair are contained in Brian Lutz's "Furniture, Form and Innovation" in *Eero Saarinen: Shaping the Future*, Eeva-Liisa Pelkonen and Donald Albrecht, eds. (Yale University Press, 2006). Vladimir Nabokov's description of his writing day is from a *Playboy* interview (January 1964).

12. Our Time

The satirical article "Report Confirms No Need to Make New Chairs for the Time Being" is from *The Onion* (posted July 15, 2014). Ralph Caplan is quoted in "His Perspective, Chairs as Symbols of Civilization and Culture" in *Chair*. The Pollock quote on designing the Knoll executive chair is contained in Kelsey Keith, "Charles Pollock (1930–2013)," *Artforum* (February 21, 2014). The observations on monobloc chairs by John Dunnigan, Marco Velardi, and Jasper Morrison are from e-mails to the author; Andrew Morrison's comments were made in conversation. The monobloc chair has not been the subject of academic study, but a good overview is provided by Alice Rawsthorn in "Celebrating the Everyday of Chairs," *The New York Times* (February 4, 2007). The "Tupperware container" quote is from Hank Stuever's "Just Resin; The Humble Plastic Chair Is Always at Home," *The Washington Post* (May 31, 2001). Jasper Morrison discusses his work in *Everything but the Walls* (Lars Müller Publishers, 2002).

ACKNOWLEDGMENTS

This book had its genesis when I read a press release about a new chair designed by Tadao Ando. I want to thank Eric Wills, my supportive editor at *Architect*, for encouraging me to pursue the subject in a magazine article that ultimately led to this book. Melissa Shelton at Carl Hansen & Søn was helpful in arranging for me to see—and sit in—the Ando chair. As the book unfolded, I sat in many more chairs, and I would like to thank Linda F. Kasper at the Knoll Museum, Karen V. Nichols and Ben Wintner at Michael Graves Design Group, and Jodee Cuddihy of Pompanoosuc Mills in Philadelphia, who patiently allowed me to try out several Diffrient task chairs. The staff at Design Within Reach in SoHo, where I tried the Air-Chair, was particularly accommodating.

I want to acknowledge John Dunnigan, not only for making two armchairs that have afforded me a great deal of pleasure over the years, but also for sharing his thoughtful observations about furniture design during a morning conversation in Providence, and not least for drawing my attention to the monobloc plastic chair. A belated thanks to the late Peter Joseph, who introduced me to Dunnigan's work and provided an early opportunity to write about furniture in a catalogue essay for his gallery. My old friend Andrew Morrison gave me the considered benefit of his many years of experience in designing furniture. Thanks to Jasper Morrison for sharing his thoughts on monobloc chairs, and to Alberto Perazza of Magis, which manufactures the Air-Chair. My appreciation to the magazine editors Marco Velardi and Martin C. Pedersen for their observations. Thanks to Laura Holland at Hickory Chair. My Penn colleague Nathan Sivin suggested several useful sources on Chinese chairs, and also clarified some Chinese terms. Michael Podmaniczky was generous in sharing his knowledge of Samuel Gragg and the Elastic Chair, and Robert Adam provided interesting material on the klismos. Thanks also to Dame Elizabeth Estève-Coll, and to Christopher Wilk of the Victoria and Albert Museum for his observations on Anton Lorenz. My McGill colleague Vikram Bhatt recounted his experience of the *jhoola* swing. My wife, Shirley Hallam, partner in many chair acquisitions over the years, cast a critical eye on my writing and also suggested the monobloc/flip-flops analogy. Thanks also to my agent, Andrew Wylie; to my editor, Eric Chinski; and to Laird Gallagher, Rodrigo Corral, and all the folks at FSG.

INDEX

Page numbers in *italics* refer to illustrations.